A History of Progressive Music and Youth Culture

Studies in Criticality

Shirley R. Steinberg
General Editor

Vol. 531

The Counterpoints series is part of the Peter Lang Education list.
Every volume is peer reviewed and meets
the highest quality standards for content and production.

PETER LANG
New York • Bern • Berlin
Brussels • Vienna • Oxford • Warsaw

Dennis Carlson

A History of Progressive Music and Youth Culture

Phishing in America

Edited by Shirley R. Steinberg
with Michael MacDonald and Robert Lake

PETER LANG
New York • Bern • Berlin
Brussels • Vienna • Oxford • Warsaw

Library of Congress Cataloging-in-Publication Data

Names: Carlson, Dennis, author. | Steinberg, Shirley R., editor.
Title: A history of progressive music and youth culture: phishing in
America / Dennis Carlson; edited by Shirley R. Steinberg;
with Michael MacDonald & Robert Lake.
Description: [First.] | New York: Peter Lang, 2020.
Series: Counterpoints: studies in criticality; v. 531 | ISSN 1058-1634
Includes bibliographical references.
Identifiers: LCCN 2020002993 (print) | LCCN 2020002994 (ebook)
ISBN 978-1-4331-7689-0 (hardback: alk. paper)
ISBN 978-1-4331-7694-4 (paperback: alk. paper) | ISBN 978-1-4331-7695-1 (ebook pdf)
ISBN 978-1-4331-7696-8 (epub) | ISBN 978-1-4331-7697-5 (mobi)
Subjects: LCSH: Rock music—Social aspects—United States—History. |
Counterculture—United States. | Phish (Musical group)
Classification: LCC ML3918.R63 C37 2020 (print) | LCC ML3918.R63 (ebook) |
DDC 782.42166—dc23
LC record available at https://lccn.loc.gov/2020002993
LC ebook record available at https://lccn.loc.gov/2020002994
DOI 10.3726/b16488

Bibliographic information published by **Die Deutsche Nationalbibliothek**.
Die Deutsche Nationalbibliothek lists this publication in the "Deutsche
Nationalbibliografie"; detailed bibliographic data are available
on the Internet at http://dnb.d-nb.de/.

The paper in this book meets the guidelines for permanence and durability
of the Committee on Production Guidelines for Book Longevity
of the Council of Library Resources.

© 2020 Peter Lang Publishing, Inc., New York
29 Broadway, 18th floor, New York, NY 10006
www.peterlang.com

All rights reserved.
Reprint or reproduction, even partially, in all forms such as microfilm,
xerography, microfiche, microcard, and offset strictly prohibited.

Printed in the United States of America

This book is dedicated to those who believe that there is but one home for us all, the planet Earth; that there is but one race of people, the human race; and that through music, the universal language, we are inspired to a greater awareness of our common bond and called to a more concerted commitment to action as global citizens facing an uncertain future.

Contents

Acknowledgments by Shirley R. Steinberg — ix
Acknowledgments by Kent Peterson — xi
No Ghost Stories Here: Foreword by Shirley R. Steinberg — xiii

Introduction Finding Phish: Music and the Education of a Counterculture — 3

1 Bebop Beginnings — 11

2 Phishy Folk — 37

3 Phish and the Spirit of Woodstock — 53

4 (Not) Dead Phish — 115

About the Team — 145

Acknowledgments

Much thanks to Robert Lake and Michael MacDonald, who assisted in going through Dennis Carlson's notes and chapters ... great scholars who were able to help finish the organization of the book. Shout-outs to musicians Phil Anderson and David Hirschman who made suggestions and comments on the early drafts. Much love and appreciation for Ron Clemons, Dennis's dear friend/brother, who worked with Kent Peterson to put together images and designs for the book. Kent, our gratitude and deepest love for sharing Dennis with us all.

—Shirley R. Steinberg

Dennis Carlson and Kent Peterson

Acknowledgments

In retrospect, Dennis was ill from the moment he conceived this book. We were simply not cognizant of that fact yet. By the time he eventually sought medical attention, we were greeted with the news of bladder cancer, stage four with metastasis to his bones. He had been working on this book project for just under two years when the oncologist told him he had maybe 12 months more to live. And thus, began the frantic race to finish what we had been casually calling the "Phish" book for months by then.

Jimmy Sallee, a dear friend and "phishing" buddy, needs to be acknowledged as the early inspiration for Dennis writing a book on this topic. Jimmy's knowledge of the band called Phish and Dennis's curiosity about the subculture surrounding the band sparked many conversations and shared stories. Through doctor's appointments, medical scans, radiation, chemotherapy, minor surgeries, discomfort and pain, Dennis persisted daily in his writing determined to finish his final book. We took comfort in the anecdotes of other cancer patients who far outlived the estimated survival times given them by their doctors. Alas, in our case it was false hope. During his final year, as I struggled to provide him as much support as was possible, I was the beneficiary of friends who supported the both of us, sitting with him while I was away at work, providing home cooked meals and surrounding us both with love and comfort as his physical condition deteriorated.

I must acknowledge the loving assistance of Ron Clemons, Margo Sacco, Will Williamson, and Jack Liles during this time. Their support was indispensable not only to the project of this book but also to our emotional equilibrium on a daily basis. In early April 2015, thirteen months after his initial diagnosis, his blood levels began to crash. No amount of transfusions could turn the tide. With heavy hearts, we agreed with the advice of his oncologist to seek out hospice. I will never forget the look of abject bitter dejection on the face of my partner of 36 years, the love of my life, as we began the process of hospice care. He lived five days from enrollment in hospice to his last breath. And the book he so frenetically attempted to finish was almost completed. Almost. The last chapter was still unwritten. It was the most bitter of pills to swallow on top of the other inevitable indignities of end stage cancer. On the third day of hospice care, a call arrived from one of his esteemed and beloved colleagues, Shirley Steinberg. Although too weak to speak with her himself, Shirley asked that I relay to him that she would make sure that his "Phish" book would get completed. After the phone call, I told Dennis what Shirley had said. His response, "Ah, that Shirley is such a good person, what a good friend!" His voice was frail but there was such a smile on his face. It would be the last time I ever saw my beloved smile. There are simply no words to express my gratitude, admiration and love to Shirley for the gift of his final smile! I gratefully acknowledge her good work, as in a "mitzvah," for shepherding my love's last book to full completion. Her actions confirm to me that not all angels have wings and halos. I am indebted beyond expression for her selfless act of kindness and love to the both of us.

—Kent Peterson
Oxford, OH
September 2019

No Ghost Stories Here

Foreword by Shirley R. Steinberg

Proclaiming an indisputable fact, Damon Linker (2019) created shivers up the spines of those of us who understand just how essential rock n' roll is to life. Indeed, with prophetic authority, Linker assaulted us with "The coming death of just about every legend." Following the loss of Bowie, Gregg Allman, Tom Petty, Prince, and, just now, at the time of writing the preface to a book on rock n' roll's essential importance to us all, Ginger Baker's death, Linker took a 3 inch leap in asserting in just a few short years, they will all be gone: "… losses have been painful. But it's nothing compared with the tidal wave of obituaries to come. Yes, the Boomers left alive will take it hardest—these were their heroes and generational compatriots." Other than stating the obvious, Linker misses the mark in digging the mass grave of rockers. As Dennis Carlson so brilliantly captures us, we understand completely that rock n' roll underpins not music, but entire cultures. While Linker rests on this one citation that I am generously giving him, those of us who are "left," are too busy ensuring that more than just a recording legacy remains infinite … immortal. Continuing his romp into the absurd, clearly emphasizing his own proclaimed GenX ignorance (no women, no people of color), he creates his own Killing Field list of 25 or so names of those who will surely go in the next few years. Walking away from the grave, he claims only the dirt and grass stuck to his own shoes in a weak tribute to a world he doesn't realize exists.

Lucky for us all, Dennis Carlson and rock continue to exist between these pages and in the souls of those who recognize that rock n' roll was not an era, a set of fads, a special time, indeed, it never *was*, rock *is* and will continue to be. In Carlson's final book, written with passion as he suffered with illness, we discover a cultural studies *magnum opus* which promises to promote and change how we interrogate culture and music. Dennis creates a crossroads of music, theory, philosophy, and change which serves to incorporate ways in which rock continues to inform, inspire, and incite youth ... and keep the rest of us engaged in support, historicity, and rebellion.

Using Phish as the nucleus for the blending of rock, youth, and culture, he re-creates cultural studies into an inter-generational lifeforce. Dennis Carlson was/is a man who loved, loves. He fiercely loved Kent- his partner, his time serving in the Peace Corps, his students, his scholarship, his friends, pets ... indeed, I can't remember anything/one Dennis didn't love. Unlike many of his contemporaries, he was devoid of the angry cynicism of leftist scholars. Make no mistake, he was indignant about oppression, he spent his life as a champion for those who were marginalized, but Dennis used respect and love to walk his path. His love for music, for rock, and specifically, for that quirky Vermont band, Phish infected us all. His final work was dedicated to drawing together his scholarly fields of critical pedagogy and cultural studies with the band he kept in his heart and soul. Through the last decades, Phish has continued to produce sound and lyrics, complicating rock with simplicity and profundity, never closing off to one particular way of being music. Like Dennis, Phish blends styles, genre, and audiences which play to all generations. One can't pin Phish down, and that's the mark of a band which continues to progress. This hippie dippy band captured the ardor of our own cultural studies aficionado, and Dennis delineates just how this jam band reaches youth, and the rest of us.

Linker was out of touch, he didn't understand the importance of rock's legacy and future. Unlike Mark Antony, this foreword is most definitely written to praise rock, not to bury it. Enjoy this journey, relax and chill out as you share a most complex and compelling read, and play a song by Phish, give a nod to Dennis Carlson, one of the finest humans to rock the Earth. Kent, this one's for you.

— Shirley R. Steinberg
New York, NY

Reference

Linker, D. (2019). The coming death of just about every rock legend. *The Week*. August 31, 2019.

Introduction

Finding Phish

Music and the Education of a Counterculture

This book is a "history of the present" (1979, p. 31) in the language of the great social historian and genealogist of knowledge Michel Foucault. It is a history of how the present has evolved out of diverse threads and currents, and how the present is characterized by continuities and discontinuities with the past. To write a history of youth culture that links the present to the past, I have adopted a generally chronological format to lay out what I call a pre-history of Phish, by which I mean a history of music and the counterculture in America before Phish came along, and out of which Phish has emerged. In their concerts, festivals, and recorded music, Phish has acknowledged this history and its influence over the band and its loyal fans (or phans, as they are known). So in presenting a pre-history of Phish and the counterculture, I begin each chapter and sections of a chapter with the Phish connection—a song or songs that have become part of the Phish repertoire, or events and places that connect Phish with these earlier movements in music and youth culture. I move from the beats and bebop in the late 1940s through the1950s, the folk revival of the early 1960s, the counterculture and rock music of the late 1960s, the "prog. rock" movement of the

1970s in the U.K., to the Grateful Dead and Tribe culture of the 1970s through the 1990s, to the jam band Phish and its phans from the 1980s through the present.

This book tells the story of a jam band named Phish, but from the perspective of a cultural studies professor and scholar interested in how popular music impacts on youth identity formation and development. My basic argument is that as popular music has become ever more commercialized and commodified since the mid-20th century, many young people have turned elsewhere, looking for the real, the authentic,[1] and for values and commitments that are more than images and sounds manufactured to sell music without substance or depth, music that does not question or challenge "the way things are" in any substantive way.

I left Seattle in a rental car heading east on I-90, up into the Cascades and down the other side, heading toward the great Columbia River Gorge and two nights of the jam band Phish in concert at the Gorge Amphitheater. It was late July 2013, and I reminded myself that I had been studying Phish for five years. As a cultural historian of youth culture in the US, I had been working on a book on Phish and Phish fan culture for some five years at that point. I was interested in where Phish and Phish culture fit into a history of progressive music and youth countercultures, going as far back as Be Bop and the Beats, the Folk Revival of the 1950s and 1960s, the progressive rock revolution of the late 1960s and beyond, all the way up to jam band music and festivals of which Phish is the best example. More specifically I was interested in what had happened to the counterculture of the Sixties. Phish is the inheritor of that counterculture whose defining moment was Woodstock, and that was carried on further if in smaller numbers through the Grateful Dead, whose fans flocked to Phish after the Dead stopped touring in 1995. If Phish is the inheritor of the Sixties counterculture, it is also the inheritor of much more and from diverse musical genres and cultural

---

1 The opposite of inauthentic—that is, more commercialized, mass-produced, and sold to youth market niches as a package of stylized images since the mid-20th century, sold to youth market "niches"—both the music itself and the meaning it takes on and the practices with which it is associated.

traditions. The power of Phish as an educator of its fans is that it helps them make connections to a multicultural history of progressive music and youth identity formation in America.

These thoughts were in my mind as I also approached the Gorge. But the ghost of Socrates was also on my mind, and in my mind, although I was learning to keep him in check. In a class I was teaching on music and youth culture at Miami University, I had students read the beginning section of Plato's great dialogue on the proper upbringing of youth, *The Republic*, to appreciate the significance of music festivals on young people.

It begins with Socrates, along with a few friends and young men who were his students, "going down" the seven miles from Athens to its seaport city of Piraeus to witness the music festival going on there. Once he gets there he views the parade of floats representing various earth goddess groups, out of respect, but does not intend to stay for the music and all night festival. He already knows what to expect of such Dionysian productions.

Piraeus was the heart of democratic Athens, and Socrates uses it to represent all the limits and excesses of democratic life, which he fears is becoming more popular among Athenian youth. Rather than bring-up young people to fill their expected roles in the social order, to be submissive to authority, to obey their parents and the law, the youth of Piraeus were being educated by the festivals to believe in multiple, subjective truths, and to view pleasure and *eros* as ends in themselves. Pireaus was, consequently, the center of a democratic Athenian youth culture that was multicultural and that came together around festivals, like the one Socrates and his friends attended, sponsored by various earth goddess sects and movements. These festivals were, in the language of the day, Dionysian productions—something Nietzsche wrote about in distinguishing between the Dionysian and the Apollonian impulses in ancient Greek culture and in Western culture today. Dionysus was the god of festivals, wine, dancing, and the celebration of life; and Apollo was the god of order, authority, law, discipline, responsibility, duty, and so on. It just so happens that Phish's production crew is named Dionysian Productions, as one of my students pointed out to me. So that was the first link, connection, key to unlocking Phish and youth culture today. Phish concerts and festivals had something in common with the festival Socrates attended, and critics of Phish fans and youth culture today have a lot in common with Socrates' criticism of the youth of Piraeus and their "bad" influence on Athenian youth. Socrates leaves Piraeus to climb back up to Athens, where Apollo is firmly in control and where Dionysian festivals are not allowed.

A part of me will always be Socrates, the man of reason who feels out of place at the festival, the carnival. But as I approached the Columbia River Gorge and crossed over the bridge, I could not help but put Socrates away. I was struck by the sublime beauty of it all—the mighty Columbia, the cliff upon which the amphitheater was perched, the little thread of a highway climbing up toward it—and I was Nietzsche the animal, senses awake, spirit uplifted, ready for the festival to begin. If anyone deserves to be called the Phish philosopher it is Nietzsche, who believed that a reawakening of the Dionysian impulse was the only thing that could save Western culture from an Apollonian power that no longer was held in check by, no longer in a dialectic relationship with, its Other. Without a viable Dionysian "will to power," we risked sinking into a culture that valued conformity, submission to authority, and acceptance of "official" truths and ways of knowing. With the Dionysian impulse deeply repressed and "managed," modern culture, Nietzsche argued, risked losing its vitality, its creativity, its imagination and vision, and thus its capacity to transform itself and move beyond its current limits, to save the world from an Apollonian impulse out of check that was inexorably leading Western culture toward the abyss. I thought that Nietzsche would have been happy to be at the Gorge that night to see that the Dionysian impulse was not dead yet, and perhaps was coming back within a broader democratic, socially-transformative movement trying to pull us back from the abyss before it is too late.

The best Phish venues are a bit removed from civilization, in sublime natural settings, like Red Rock in Colorado and like the Gorge Amphitheater in Washington State, so that the festivities can go on into the night without disturbing any neighbors and the fans can camp out under the stars, and also so that the concert can re-connect people to the real world of nature. The Gorge Amphitheater was perched on top of the Gorge, overlooking it, with the Cascades rising in the distance, behind which the sun set in a fantastic blaze of glory. Bands do not simply perform at the Gorge Amphitheater, they provide music to a natural cyclical event unfolding, the setting of the sun. I had come as a professor engaged in writing a book about Phish and its loyal fan base which I had been following for some five years. Over the course of that time I had gone to only a half dozen Phish shows and a three-day festival, which is far fewer than the average Phish fan. In fact, many fans have been to over 100 concerts. But I was beginning to know something of the concert experience, and had begun to move from my position as observer and witness to the position of participant, getting caught up in the dance and the whole celebration of life. Along the way I also recorded some interviews with fans I met at concerts or through online blogs; and I had listened to hundreds of hours of Phish, often while in my car on long trips, including both their studio albums and recordings of live performances. This two-night event at the Gorge was to give me another experience of the real Phish, as an observer but by now also a participant observer.

I Had Come Like Socrates to Piraeus, to Witness the Dionysian Festival

I was of the Boomer generation, so I had some connection to Phish. Music, and rock music festivals like Woodstock, had played a key role in the making of middle-class youth identities in the Sixties, and making them within the context of a counterculture committed to a fundamental transformation of society. For all the naiveté and excesses of the counterculture, it did connect many relatively privileged middle class suburban high school and college youth to democratic progressive social movements and ideas. And it did offer community, a radically inclusive community where everyone is (at least ostensibly) free to be whoever they are or want to be, and simultaneously part of the whole, the event, the community coming together as a collective spirit through the rhythm and beat and words of the music and the dancing. In sum, I was interested in writing about what had happened to music and youth culture since then, and whether groups like Phish and events such as this one at the Gorge might still have the potential to educate young people in democratic progressive values and impulses and give them the opportunity to experience a real rather than merely virtual or imaginary community, one organized through practices of freedom and communalism, and the unleashing of desire—desire in all its forms, but most directly the desire of the body to run and jump and dance, and also the desire for spiritual connection.

At a Phish concert, like the one I attended in late July 2013 at the Gorge, everyone gets up and begins dancing when the band starts playing, and most don't sit down through two sets of songs and jams, letting the music and the crowd synch their body to the flow, so that the event is experienced through the dance, as a dance in which individuals both dance alone and always in relation to others, and in which the band and the fans stage their own dance of sorts, each creatively producing the event, this experience of community. But what about the music?

And that led me to an interest in situating Phish within a history of popular music—beginning in the late 1940s and the 1950s with bebop and the beats—that played a formative role in the upbringing of middle class, relatively privileged young people. Phish makes that easy because the band explicitly aims to educate its fans on this history by "covering" artists and albums from the past and by drawing upon a multicultural mix of music genres to create their own hybrid funk. After studying Phish for five years and attending a half dozen concerts along with a three-day festival (*SuperBall IX*, Watkins Glen, New York on July 1–3, 2011) I had become a participant observer, having an experience, feeling once more the feeling of being caught up in it all and the incredible positive "vibes" people were giving off.

What happens, then, in a society in which there is no dialectic between the Dionysian and the Apollonian, in which the young grow up in educational institutions and workplaces that value only the latter and do their best to suppress the former? This is the world most young people inhabit, and if our future these days is so often represented in dark, almost lifeless, post-apocalyptic terms, it is because without the Dionysian impulse, the democratic imagination is dimmed and young people abandon hope for a better, non-alienating world. I came to the

Gorge concerts, as I had come to other Phish concerts, with a bit of Socrates in me—playing the observer, the outsider, taking notes on this primal scene and then returning to my motel room to get a good night's sleep. But the spirit of Nietzsche tugged at my Boomer body, reminding me of what it had been like to attend a rock concert in the late 1960s and early 1970s, and I kicked up my feet in dance and entered into the collective flow. I remembered what Nietzsche wrote—"A day you have not danced is a day you have wasted"—and I was suddenly aware that I had wasted too many of my days. Across the years and decades, the best days were those I danced through my work—my writing and my teaching—improvising and responding to the flow, always creatively responding to the moment, always living in my body as well as my head, and always playfully performing. Dancing to music at festivals, most prominently Woodstock, was also and already a political act, not in a narrow electoral politics sense, but in sense of being about bringing on what Charles Reich (1970) called "the greening of America," a fundamental shift in consciousness that would usher in a new democratic and progressive era.

But what if the dialectic between the Apollonian and the Dionysian are no longer working? What happens to the Dionysian impulse then? One answer provided by Freud is that it is repressed (bound up) and sublimated (made to serve a more "productive" aim through work). In that case, the Dionysian pretty well disappears and is kept invisible and "in the closet." This traditional approach to managing the Dionysian impulse in young people, however, always faced resistance and so in contemporary Western cultures, the Dionysian impulse is managed and contained by providing a space for it, a space where young people can "let go," "let it all out," and then return to their "normal" lives where repression and sublimation are still the norm. This is an example of what the radical psychoanalytic philosopher Herbert Marcuse called "repressive de-sublimation" (1991, p. 56). Repressive de-sublimation is when room or space is created for a cathartic release of the Dionysian impulse in a "safe" environment so that young people can go back to their books and their offices and submit themselves once more to the authority of educational and work routines. Was that what I was seeing all around me at the Gorge Phish concert, some collective catharsis, a repressive de-sublimation that in its very excess seemed to confirm that this was a space apart and not the way the "real" world works, the world of drudgery and alienation?

I had come as a fan, wanting my own Phish experience again, and I had come as a professor, writing a book about Phish and the fan culture that has grown up around the band over the past three decades. I had begun my study of Phish some five years earlier, on a simple idea.

As someone who grew up and came of age in the 1960s, and who witnessed and was involved in the youthful counterculture of the time—combining both political activism with a new lifestyle, new values, new counter-institutions—I wondered what had happened to all that youthful idealism and even utopianism that so characterized college youth back then, and whether Phish might be the missing key to unlock an understanding of young people today.

References

Foucault, M. (1979). *Discipline and punish: The birth of the prison*. Harmondsworth, GB: Penguin Books.

Marcuse, H. (1991). *One-dimensional man: Studies in the ideology of advanced industrial society*. Boston, MA: Beacon Press.

Plato, & Allen, R. E. (2006). *The republic*. New Haven, CT: Yale University Press.

Reich, C. A. (1970). *The greening of America: How the youth revolution is trying to make America livable*. New York, NY: Random House.

Chapter One

Bebop Beginnings

Simple

Phish drummer Jon Fishman has remarked that the band's song *Simple* is probably his "favorite song in our entire repertoire" (160). Bass player Mike Gordon refers to *Simple* as an "anthemic" song for the band because it attempts to sum up what Phish is all about. *Simple* is about getting back to basics, remembering who you are. In Phish's case, *Simple* provides a simple answer, and like all simple answers, they don't tell the whole story. But simple answers can be a place to begin. The song is in fact among Phish's simplest compositions. *Simple* proclaims that "we are a bebop band," with cymbals and saxophones in the band. It hardly matters that Phish does not have saxophones or cymbals in the band. It resurrects some of the spirit of bebop. Originally crafted by Mike Gordon in 1994, the song with its riff of simple, repeated phrases with changing chords and harmonies provides a perfect vehicle for improvisation and jamming. No two performances of *Simple* have ever been the same but the riff provides a unifying structure that can be returned to again and again, to maximize improvisation without getting lost in chaos. By making *Simple* a prominent and recurring song in their repertoire, Phish directs its loyal fans back to an earlier generation of music and youth culture with the suggestion that "we" (the Phish community) are all inheritors of a bebop legacy, that the education of a Phish fan needs to include heavy doses of jazz history, and the bebop era is a good place to start.

Phish's jazz connections began in the mid-1980s when the group was living in a house in Winooski, Vermont. Around the corner a club named *Sneakers* featured Tuesday night local jazz. Phish eventually found employment as a back up horn section for local musicians James Harvey and Dave Grippo, under the name "Johnny B. Fishman Jazz Ensemble." During the first decade of performing, Phish regularly introduced jazz standards by Duke Ellington, Charles Mingus, and Charley Parker as vehicles for jamming. These jazz standards were gone from Phish's set lists by the mid-1990s, as their sounds, rhythms and beats, and improvisational style became part of the Phish sound fusion. Beginning in 1990, Phish added a cover of *Manteca* to its recurring repertoire that continued through to the band's current incarnation as Phish 3.0. *Manteca*, by the self-proclaimed "King of Bebop" Dizzy Gillespie, is an interesting choice. Gillespie introduced a radically new sound in the fall of 1947, and it pointed to what Gillespie hoped was bebop's future as a dynamic force for change in America. Bebop was to be a music that "shakes people awake," shakes them into action, wakes them up to what is going on in America. The only lyrics in *Manteca* are "I'll never go back to Georgia," and Gillespie sings it as an inside joke for the fans, the ones who would get it because they know what happened when he and his orchestra had been on a tour of the South in July and August 1945 billed as "The Hepsations of 1945." The trouble was that bebop was almost unheard of in the South so there was no fan base waiting to welcome the band. Gillespie saw it as his job to create a fan base, although that would prove difficult. In the Jim Crow South the band could only play to Black audiences and typically in high school auditoriums and local theatres. The audiences were used to bands to whose music they could dance. They liked the predictable rhythms and melodies of swing and blues bands, and they were almost completely unschooled in the bebop revolution that was going on in

New York and other big cities in the North. The music seemed too fast-paced, too agitating, too hard to follow let alone dance to it.

Dizzy

Gillespie observed in his 1979 memoir, *To Be or Not to Bop*: "They couldn't dance to the music, they said. But I could dance to it. I could dance my ass off to it. They could have too, if they had tried" (2009, p. 223). Indeed, from Gillespie's perspective, jazz had to make you move or it wasn't working: "It should always be rhythmic enough to make you want to move" (Gillespie, 2009, p. 223). It was just that bebop made you move in a different way, in a more improvisational expression of movement and flow, as the music moves you. That was the difference between bebop and the blues or later rock n' roll. Bebop dancing was an improvised self-expression without rules or even partners as such, each person moving in their own space but participating in a common "groove." Black youth in the South were not ready for that kind of music, Gillespie learned, because they had no experience of freedom and self-production. Gillespie would return to New York City from the Southern tour and put it behind him. But he would continue to wrestle with a central conflict and tension in his music and life. On the one hand, he wanted to be popular and accepted by a big and growing fan base, and that drove him to think about how to make bebop more danceable, because that was the only way to reach young people. On the other hand, he was an artist and he believed bebop was supposed to educate people, to push them beyond their comfort zones, and not just to entertain them.

He wrote of the 1945 Southern tour, "we never carried big crowds because jazz is strictly an art form" and bebop audiences were about "participating in an art form" (Gillespie, 2009, p. 230). Gillespie decided that the trick would be to make bebop more danceable and thus more popular without at the same time following the lead of those who "manufactured meaningless tinsel rolling off an assembly line" (p. 230). He would not bend on that, and so would have to teach young people to dance to bebop's improvisational style, to un-discipline the body in order to free it from its mental servitude. Gillespie negotiated a twin tension in the development of progressive music youth culture: trying to mediate between popularity and artistry, and between a broad public fan base and smaller, more artistically open, and more loyal fan base. This form of progressive aesthetic youth education has played a role in Phish's development as a band and their cultivation of a fan community. Centrally important is their claims to authenticity, that vaguely defined but centrally important notion in music and youth culture—associated with the proposition that bands and their fans are not just producing and consuming "fluff," without substance, like cotton candy that tastes good but quickly dissolves in your mouth leaving nothing behind. They are exploring new social and artistic territory in the creation of new sound-meanings.

In the fall of 1947, *Manteca* was created and performed for the first time, and it may be taken as Gillespie's own response to this tension in his life and music between jazz as art and as popular culture entertainment. His response was to fuse African American jazz with its more rhythmic brother, Afro-Cuban jazz, creating a new sound that was a crowd-pleaser and guaranteed to get people up and moving. For some time, Gillespie had been interested in Afro-centrism, and looking for ways to make bebop more consciously Afro-centric. He found what he was looking for in Chano Pozo, who was working as a bongo drummer for dance companies around New York. He had been raised in the Cuban *lucimi* faith, with roots in West African spiritual rituals and chanting and drum playing traditions and Gillespie immediately saw how Pozo's rhythms and beats could be woven into his own and quickly hired him.

Gillespie along with George Russell (a professor of music) and Pozo all contributed to the first Afro-Cuban bebop song, *Cubana Be-Cubana Bop*, of which Gillespie would observe, "it was the most successful collaboration I ever [sic] seen with three people" (Shipton, 1999, p. 199). It was performed for the first time with Gillespie's big band at Carnegie Hall on September 29, 1947, to critical acclaim and to the audience's delight. Shortly thereafter, the trio collaborated to produce *Manteca*, and it slowly began to replace *Cubana Be-Cubana Bop* as the band's signature Afro-Cuban song. In both songs, Chano provided the pounding bongo beats and rhythms, and shared in leading improvisational sections. With Gillespie's approval Pozo also began wearing brightly colored African and Cuban-African dress to concerts (something Gillespie would later do as well), and he began chanting in words that were gibberish to everyone else. The effect was electrifying and a bit too exotic, especially for middle class concert hall audiences. During a concert at Boston Symphony Hall shortly thereafter, Pozo was featured dressed as an African native, chanting and drumming, taking the band and the audience back to a pre-European African rhythm and beat that was the origins of jazz, before it became Europeanized as "cool" jazz and relegated to coffee houses. Pozo and Gillespie both appreciated putting on a good show, and the new Afro-Cuban sounds, along with Pozo and Gillespie's theatrics and wittiness, brought it all together in a dramatic and powerful musical event.

But not everyone loved the new sound and the emphasis upon performativity—that is, putting on a good, exciting, fast-paced show. Nor did they appreciate Pozo's overt display of Africanness. The audience in Boston included a good number of middle class African Americans who were assimilationist in their cultural politics, just wanting to fit into and be accepted within the dominant White culture. As Russell recalled, "the black people in the audience were embarrassed by it" (Shipton, 1999, p. 200). When Pozo came on stage they began to laugh, rather nervously, "the cultural snow job had worked so ruthlessly that for the black race in America at the time its native culture was severed from it completely. They were taught to be ashamed of it"(Shipton, 1999, p. 200). As for the mostly White middle class who attended the Carnegie Hall concert that fall, and certainly for "serious" music critics, the Afro-Cuban dress, the joking, the theatrics were "inexcusable"—such was the judgment of *New York Times* music critic Michael Levin, who wrote the day after the concert that showmanship is one thing, but that "this doesn't mean that he [Gillespie] has the license to stand on a platform doing bumps, grinds, and in general often acting like a darn fool" (Haddix, 2013, p. 112). The trouble, perhaps, was that Gillespie associated being taken "seriously" with playing at symphony halls wanting to be liked by the high culture music establishment—where bebop and improvisation always would be an exotic diversion from the European classical canon. So long as bebop bands "dressed up" in tuxedoes and downplayed racial identity, they could perform at Carnegie Hall and Boston's Symphony Hall. But as soon as they began to incorporate elements of an authentic jazz, and showmanship, the high culture fans and music critics would turn on them. That did not sway Gillespie from continuing to promote Pozo and what they called "cubop" (McCrae, 1989, p. 48) music because that's what the people wanted to hear.

In early December 1948, while drinking at a bar in uptown Manhattan, Pozo got into a fight with another patron and was fatally shot. His untimely and tragic death was a blow to the band and to Gillespie personally. But *Manteca* stayed in the band's list of most popular songs. Gillespie remarked: "I learned that most of the putdowns of our music came from a small elite, not the masses of people because everywhere we went large crowds flocked to hear us, even down South" (Gillespie, 2009, p. 342). Bebop did become a mass phenomenon in the late 1940s and early 1950s in the U.S. and *Manteca* was finally recorded as an extended "Suite" for release on a 1954 LP. Jazz was quickly migrating to the LP format since it could more easily accommodate complex and improvisational jams. Top forty mainstream music would be formatted for 78 and then 45 RPMs, and Gillespie and other bebop artists decided not to play in that highly-commercialized game of writing hits for the *culture industry* (Adorno, 2001). The LP provided the possibility of recording entire live concerts, which were after all what jazz was all about—returning to the specificity of a unique performance that can only happen once, in interaction with a real audience. Fans attended a Dizzy Gillespie big band concert wondering what would be on the set list that night, and whether the jams would flow in exciting new directions.

In 1948, Gillespie took his orchestra to Los Angeles where bebop culture was a bandwagon for suburban kids as well as inner-city gangs. Among many middle-class youth, bebop became self-parody, an exaggerated image and style. According to Barry McCrae, "opportunists began to sell complete uniforms for the aspiring bop fan—berets, 'bop glasses', and even comic, spotted ties that were dubbed 'bop bow ties'" (McCrae, 1989, p. 51). Gillespie himself promoted bebop style—as a stylized performance, a look, a way of walking, and a way of talking—and presented himself as the exemplar of this style. To identify with bebop culture, people needed to look bebop, to self-identify as members of bebop underground and thus a counter-force in America, part of a new culture of young people who were taking control of their own identities and imagining a new multicultural America. If bebop was anything, it was a movement that drew White, Black, and Latina/o youth, as well as working class and middle class youth, together across their differences, without dissolving or assimilating those differences, in a common love of bebop rhythms and beats and bebop anthems like *Manteca* (Kun, 2005). For White-identified young people, bebop taught them, or reminded them, of a very basic truth: their music, when you go back far enough, is African much more than European; and if music never really can be separated from a cultural legacy, Whites in American are hybrid subjects indeed. "White" as a racial category of pure, European-based identity, was radically called into question by bebop as White fans and music groups (like Phish and most of its fans) came to recognize themselves as inheritors of Black and Latin musical histories. When Whites began listening to and dancing to Black music like bebop and later rock n' roll, the dominant or hegemonic White culture felt threatened, and well it should have. Once bebop youth were all moving to the same rhythms and beats, they could begin to imagine themselves as being on the same side, as they would need to be in the civil rights battles to come. They would all need to learn how to beat the drums of change. Bebop's politics was not overt and in your face, but rather consisted in a set of commitments to using music to free young people to lead a cultural revolution. In his memoir, Gillespie observed that the drum, the most basic and powerful African instrument, was banned under slavery in the U.S. This "was very smart of the slavemasters because you could talk with the drums and foment revolution and uprisings" (Gillespie, 2009, p. 484). African drums and bebop bands would, he hoped, lead young people around the world to speak up, stand up, and rise up, and to take their futures back.

Bebop artists like Gillespie enjoyed great success in bringing this new subversive music to American youth, crossing class, race/ethnicity, and gender divides. In the process they sowed seeds that would begin to bear fruit during the civil rights and anti-war movements of the 1960s. But this story of bebop, of great jazz artists and bands and how they participated in the "making" of a youth culture, is only one side of the story and it overemphasizes the role of big bands as the formative agent in change. In fact, it would be more accurate to say that Gillespie and others merely re-worked and artistically developed music forms and cultural developments being created by young people at the time. In all the boroughs of New York City by 1945, the oft-cited beginning of the bebop era, local bands, often affiliated with youth gangs, were blaring their music into the night, a loud disruptive note to mark the end of the swing era, with its smooth sounds, conventional styles, and capacity for commercialization. As Eric Schneider has observed of the bebop gangs of New York, "you could go anywhere in the city and even if you ran into a rival gang, you could still identify with them ... Bop culture united gang members even as ethnicity and place divided them" (Schneider, 2001, p. 137).

It was Black gangs that originated bebop and in the few years leading up to 1945 they were the only ones doing it. For them, bebop was about speaking back to power and reclaiming an African heritage, it was a vehicle of defiance and anti-assimilationism. They would not, like their parent's generation, be submissive and quiet and ashamed of their Africanness. While each neighborhood and borough of New York City had its unique sound and bebop bands, their own individual expressions of bebop, as Imanu Baraka has observed, all shared one thing in common, a "harsh, anti-assimilationist sound" that spoke of resistance and self-affirmation among Black males who were getting tired of being beaten down and were prepared to fight back (Schneider, 2001, p. 138). As a sign of their rejection of the dominant culture's version of standard English, they invented a whole language of their own, new styles of clothes that made them stand out from the cultural norm, and a whole new way of walking or "bopping" that was self-assertive. A member of the *Brooklyn Mau Maus* gang (a reference to the Mau Mau insurrection going on in Kenya against British colonial rule) remembers: "We walked down the street like we owned it ... loosely swinging our shoulders, hips, and knees, bobbing and weaving to our own individual rhythm" (Schneider, 2001, p. 143). This was a walk that announced itself and made the racial Other visible, as a bopper who had to be reckoned with. Bebop had become a complex and multi-faceted counterculture for a growing number of young Blacks in the city by the end of the 1940s.

On the Road

A passage from the Jack Kerouac's novel, *On the Road* (1957) was posted prominently at the entrance to a 2003 Phish festival in Limestone, Maine—a festival simply named IT.

> Here's a guy and everyboy's there, right? Up to him to put down what's on everybody else's mind. He starts the first chorus, then lines up his ideas, people, yeah, yeah, but get it, and then rises to his fate and has to blow equal to it. All of a sudden somewhere in the middle of the chorus he gets IT—everybody looks up and knows; they listen; he picks it up and carries. Time stops. He's filling empty space with the substance of our lives, confessions of his bellybutton strain, remembrance of ideas, rehashes of old blowing. He has to blow across bridges and come back and do it with such infinite feeling soul-exploratory for the tune of the moment that everybody knows its not the tune that counts but IT. (p. 170)

The lines are spoken by the character Dean Moriarty, who is based on a friend of Kerouac named Neil Cassady, and they are spoken about a bebop saxophonist Dean and Sal have heard perform in a band. The whole tone and feel of *On the Road* is an attempt to represent the basic elements of bebop jazz and its improvisational, rhythmic flow, in prose. According to Phish biographer, Parke Puterbaugh, Kerouac's style of writing is "spontaneous bop prosody," in which he wrote without correction or even paragraph breaks, provided a model for Phish in "getting out of one's way" (2009, p. 125) to create and perform music—letting it flow without too much deliberate forethought. This is, indeed, the key to unpacking the meaning of IT and the contributions of the beats to the making of a counterculture.

The bebop revolution was spreading among White youth by the late 1940s—in working class ethnic urban neighborhoods in particular, but also among a growing group of middle class urban bohemians, like those that were re-shaping the cultural landscape of Greenwich Village around bebop cultural styles and bebop clubs, and connecting to the jazz joints of Harlem. Kerouac had taken the word "beat" from the streets of New York, from young bebop gang members, particularly Black gangs, in which the word was used to refer to being "beat down," but also referred to beating back, to that low, assertive sounds of the bebop drum (Watson, 1998, p. 3). In sum, it signified a generation that was "growing up absurd," as the social critics Paul Goodman (1960) said, both beat down and beating back. The novel is based on journals kept by Kerouac of three road trips he took between 1947 and 1950. In July 1947, while Gillespie's band was putting the finishing touches on *Manteca*, Kerouac (who in the novel is Sal Paradise) leaves New York City with $50 in his pocket, hitch-hiked across the country to connect with Cassady (Dean Moriarty in the novel). Along the road, the two were joined, off and on, by the two other major beat literary figures—Allen Ginsberg as Carlos Marx and William Burroughs as Old Bull Lee. Together and alone they engaged in a journey in search of IT across a godless, commercialized American landscape, where the only really interesting people "are the mad ones, the ones who are mad to live, mad to talk, mad to be saved, desirous of everything at the same time" (Kerouac, p. 5).

On the Road offers Phish connections galore. First, the real Neal Cassady, the model for Dean Moriarty, would, in 1964, be the driver of the Merry Prankster's psychedelically-designed bus "Furthur" (as in taking it further) on another cross-country trip that announced the coming of the counterculture in communities across America—a bit early it turned out. Cassady died in 1969, basically worn out by two decades of partying on the road. But his spirit was revived in 1997 when the Merry Pranksters, with their leader for more than three decades, author Ken Kesey, made one last roadtrip, driving Furthur (now also the name of what was left of the Grateful Dead band under the leadership of Bob Weir and Phil Lesch) to the Rock and Roll Hall of Fame in Cleveland, where Further was to go on display as an icon of the 1960s counterculture. On their way to Cleveland, the Pranksters showed up at a Phish concert at Darien Lake in New York to practice their own brand of pranksterism on stage. Cassady was a prankster in a subversive sense, that is, disrupting what is expected or scripted and breaking out of the "normal" way of thinking and acting, and Phish always have practiced their own brand of pranksterism at concerts that has direct connections to Cassady. But more than this, the character of Moriarty as the beat anti-hero in search of god and finding it in surrendering to the moment and the flow of a bebop jam, of living on the road, listening to bebop in different towns and cities across America late into the night, is a romanticized representation of the Phish fan.

Several years ago at Miami University, where I teach, *On the Road* was selected as the book all entering frosh would read together and discuss in their classes, a tribute to the staying power of a book now over six decades removed from Kerouac's America. This suggests that while things have changed a great deal since the mid-20th century, it is still possible to see continuities with that earlier time. Enough remains the same, or has further developed, so that young people can still relate to the novel's themes and characters. In recent years, when *On the Road* is used as a text in college classes in literature, cultural studies, and youth studies, it often is deconstructed and critiqued for its misogynistic treatment of women, and for its valorization of "real men" over "weak" and "effeminate" men. The road gets positioned as a masculine space, populated by men who live above and outside of conventional morality and sexual identity lines yet never question conventional gender norms or the cult of masculinity. This cult of the real man, as Dean and Sal perform it, gives them free reign to roam with their buddies, engage in homosocial and homosexual bonding, and treat most all women as prostitutes, sexual possessions, and stay-at-home wives.

The irony is that the beats, as sexual libertines, were significantly ahead of their time in accepting homosexuality and homosexuals without judgment, as expressing of a natural sexual diversity. Indeed, two of the central characters in the novel are openly gay: Carlos Marx as the real-life Alan Ginsberg and Old Bull Lee as William Burroughs. Furthermore, Kerouac, Cassady, and Ginsberg all had sexual relations with each other at some point, Ginsberg as an openly gay man and Kerouac and Cassady as bisexuals (Gattghan, 2004, pp. 452–453; Ginsberg, 1993, pp. 358, 399–430).

Even exclusively heterosexual males in beat culture could at least entertain the idea of homosexual desire for their buddies, and this was a breakthrough in youth culture in an age when homosexuality was still classified as a mental illness, a sin, and a perversion in "straight" society. At the same time, the beats were less accepting of "effeminacy." At one point in their cross-country journeys, Dean and Sal hitch a ride with someone Sal describes as a "tall, thin fag ... who drove with extreme care." Dean whispers in Sal's ear that the driver has a "fag Plymouth" with no power, an "effeminate car" (p. 170). This is a telling statement, indicating just how much the dominant cult of masculinity in the beat era and continuing through the Muscle Car era of the 1970s, was invested in masculinizing automobiles and judging some to be effeminate, something no "real" man would drive.

While the cult of masculinity still has its appeals to young men today, the "hippie" counterculture movement of the 1960s dramatically shifted the meaning of masculinity, and Phish fans today are arguably more influenced by the counterculture reconstruction of masculinity as softer, more peaceful, even androgynous. The counterculture countered the image of the "real" man with the image of the "gentle" man, wearing a t-shirt with a peace sign on it, driving an "effeminate," under-powered Volkswagen Beetle or bus. It is significant that Phish includes one gender-bending member, the drummer John Fishman, who always performs in the same polka-dot dress and men's work boots. His unshaven face makes it clear that he is not cross-dressing, but gender bending, subverting the normal performance of masculinity to reveal its arbitrariness. When Phish performed at the Gorge Amphitheater in Washington State in July 2013, I noticed several men dressed as Fishman, and one father paraded around with his twelve year old son who wore a Fishman dress. Also, most male Phish fans do not view women as only sexual objects at Phish concerts—at least in principle if not always in fact—but as fans, equal in every way to any other fan, here to see the show not to be picked up.

At the same time, it is clear that some things have not changed since the beats gender-wise. The road is still a masculinized space, and males (particularly White, middle class males) are still privileged to be able to go on the road, living a wild, "mad" life in pursuit of ecstasy, without many real or lasting consequences. This is a privilege few women fans have or take for granted, which is why the "typical" Phish fan (if I can be excused for using a word that is highly suspicious, and rightfully so, among Phish fans) is a White, male, college student or college graduate in his twenties or early thirties, much like the Kerouac's cast of characters—except for Dean, who is a genuine working class bebop fan.

As for as sexual identity and difference, many male Phish fans share the beats libertine and accepting attitude. Recently, a fan-produced t-shirt has been circulating in the Phish community with the words "Gay for Trey" printed on it, implying the wearer would gladly have a sexual relationship with Trey Anastasio, the band's unofficial leader if he should ever ask. In this case, the wearer of the t-shirt also proclaims "I'm straight," and that it's okay for "straight" men to acknowledge "gay" desire. In this case, the attitude is actually more like the attitude of the beats than the attitude of the gay rights movement. Phish fans, like the beats, prefer ambiguity to fixity of identity. This also means that members of the LGBTQ community were welcomed into the Phish fan community so long as they do not separate themselves too much by that identity. Phish identity in the eyes of many fans is supposed to unite fans across race, gender, sexual, and class differences. Ironically this serves to mute some fan identities as they are assimilated into a meta-identity as members of the Phish community, similar in some ways to the early Pauline Christian communities where everyone, no matter what their race or ethnicity or status was welcome into the "community of Christ." This is not necessarily a bad way to build community, so long as differences are not erased or made invisible in the process. Kerouac had hoped that the beats could be such a community that brought American youth together across their differences, and it is possible to find the same hope in the idea of a Phish community, even if the imaginary is not yet the real.

IT

Kerouac, like many others who identified with the beat movement, was deeply influenced by Buddhism, or more accurately Americanized versions of Buddhism that were circulating within bohemian social networks in the late 1940s and early 1950s. Kerouac immersed himself in the study of Buddhism by 1953, when he was re-drafting *On the Road*. He brought this Buddhist turn in his thinking to center stage, without making it explicit—since the novel is set in the late 1940s before its characters knew anything about Buddhism. It is possible to trace a rather direct path from Kerouac's appropriation of Buddhism in the 1950s, to the re-appropriation of Buddhism (along with Hinduism) in the late 1960s by the Woodstock Nation, to the living legacy of this appropriation and re-appropriation of Eastern Spirituality in Phish culture. Kerouac, like most beats in the early 1950s, was not a serious disciple of Buddhism. Nevertheless, he began to think that Buddhism might provide a space for constructing an alternative culture in America, one that opened a path to personal enlightenment and through that to social transformation. As the literary historian Micheal Dittman (2004, 2007) has observed, Kerouac began to reformulate *On the Road* around an examination of two seemingly-competing Buddhist principles, both of which he believed must be affirmed simultaneously in pursuit of enlightenment or IT.

The first of these principles or truths is that of *Tathagata*, which implies a state of having no attachments to either other people or the material world—a state of letting everything and everyone go and surrendering to the eternal moment, here and now, and to the flow of time from one moment to another (Dittman, 2007, p. 53). This is the principle that primarily motivates the character Dean, and that Sal finds so compelling and essential in learning to reawaken the human soul and imagination from the mind-numbing effects of modern life. It returns people to the "real," in the Lacanian sense, the actual material and social world that is the field of our experience and in which we act, or don't act. This is, from a Buddhist perspective, the only reality there, but because it is a flowing, always moving reality, to live in the real requires letting go of everything that is not present at hand. Kerouac believed that if it is not coupled or countered with another attitude, that of *Bodhisattva*, having no attachments and letting everything go can lead to narrow self-absorption. This principle implied for Kerouac balancing the path of personal bliss as letting go of all attachments with the path of engaging in the world, here and now in order to ease human suffering. This too is a path to IT—enlightenment—but one that links personal enlightenment and "bliss" with engagement in struggles against human suffering and domination (Dittman, 2007, p. 53). In the words of Kerouac scholar Matt Theado, this path to Buddhism helped Kerouac and other beats identify with "the condition of people who do not have what they want or have what they do not want, who sorrow and grieve, or who are ill" (2000, p. 124). *On the Road* weaves both of these principles and paths together, particularly in the character of Sal, while Dean represents both the power and the limits of a life lived according to *Tathagata* alone. Dean consequently emerges from the novel as a deeply-flawed if still heroic beat character.

Dean is heroic and enlightened to Kerouac precisely because of his letting go, his detachment from everything but the moment and the people he is relating to at the moment. He has detached himself from worrying about living and throws himself into the process of living, and breaks through all conventions in pursuit of IT. He is heroic within the context of an American middle class, White American culture that had lost its soul and lost its way in pursuit of the false gods of material possessions and social status. For his part, Dean thinks of himself as a student, still learning IT, which is why he is drawn to the beat intellectuals for what they could teach him—in particular Carlos Marx, and the real-life Allen Ginsberg, with whom he had a sexual as well as intellectual relationship.

He also reads as a path to enlightenment. When Sal finds him in Denver on one road trip, before he sees Dean, Sal notices the book on the table, a volume in Marcel Proust's *Remembrances of Things Past*, and he knows Dean must be around. Everything Dean stood for and believed in seemed opposed to the attitude of that classic piece of literature, with the narrator retreating into his own past and living in it again, but selectively and from the perspective of a life already lived. Proust's novel obviously presents Dean with a different way of living and finding meaning in life that is almost the total opposite of the path he has chosen, of letting go of the past and the future and living now. Perhaps this is because Dean's past—of poverty, reform school and prison, living on the streets and drifting from one job, town, and woman is full of despair and suffering—is so starkly different from the refined, bourgeois characters Proust wrote about. But Dean must be drawn to reading Proust because Proust knows something about time, and for Dean time is what IT is all about. Of one character whom Dean identifies as having IT, he remarks: "he's never hung-up, he goes every direction, he lets it all out, and he knows time" (Kerouac, 1957, p. 106).

To know time, from Dean's perspective, is to know that we inhabit an eternal moment within a real world, in a moving timeframe. There is no yesterday or tomorrow, only the eternal, ever-changing present. In such a world, we have to learn how to "Surrender to the Flow" (to borrow the name of an online Phish fanzine), and also learn how to direct the flow and open an improvising path laid down by walking or jamming. This Buddhist conception of time is captured well in the Phish song *The Moma Dance*, with its repeated refrain, "the moment ends and I feel winds," the winds of time that push us further down the road. This is an understanding of time that returns to what the social-psychoanalytic theorist Jacques Lacan called the "real," the actual material and temporal plane of existence, as distinct from the "imaginary" of remembered events, dreams, and hopes for the future (Lacan, 2006). IT consequently involves a radical reengagement with the "real" as the authentic ground of being, and a recognition of real time, which requires that we always improvise a response to an ever-changing, always unique situation at hand. This is why Kerouac's first draft of *On the Road* was improvisational writing over several days, letting the words flow. In an improvisational life, no two performances are ever quite the same, and you need to have a good sense of what is flowing around you, where opportunities exist to change or direct the flow. This is the quintessence of beat wisdom about time.

Interestingly, this is not an individualistic conception of time, of people who know time on their own. In fact, while Dean seems very self-absorbed and self-centered, he always describes IT as a way of transcending the ego through an experience of connectivity to everyone and everything, a peak experience that is spiritual in nature. Kerouac suggested, with great irony, that what went on at bebop jazz concerts was more deeply spiritual than what went on in most houses of worship, and be believed that young people were turning to bebop to recover a lost spirituality, to compensate for the de-spiritualization of the life-world in contemporary American culture. Like Nietzsche, Kerouac and other beats were of the opinion that modern society had killed god—at least as "he" was understood in the churches—even if many people (a declining number it turned out) continued to profess belief in religious dogma. Nietzsche's answer to an organized religious life lacking in spirit, was the re-spiritualization of the life-world, a theme taken up not only by the beats but also by youth counterculture in the 1960s.

The spiritual dimension of the IT experience is something that Phish understand well. Phish fans I have had conversations with often speak eloquently of this spiritual meaning of the concert experience. They describe times when everyone was on the same "vibe" or "groove," part of the same becoming. In a similar way, fans may describe being on the road with Phish as a spiritual quest or journey. When "Mister Miner," a Phish fan blogger and enthusiast, wrote an essay on the meaning of the quote from *On the Road* posted at the entrance to the band's 2003 IT festival, he drew parallels between the saxophonist in the quote and Phish when they are "hitting a sacred stride" and "transcending their art form." At these times, he wrote, "those quiet moments of your soul, when the band is soaring into alternative universes and the energy enters you like osmosis ... you are just part of IT." The effect, is to "fill up your reserves of inspiration, energy, and adrenaline"—a kind of spiritual shock treatment.

The search for a lost spirituality is a recurring narrative among young people, particularly among White, middle class youth, whose oppression (in the face of privilege), is alienation from an authentic spiritual connectedness to other people and the life-world. Of course, it is easy to pass judgment on privileged youth on the road in search of spiritual highs, as if they had nothing better to do. In a recent essay on Kerouac's *On the Road* and the character of Dean as a romantic anti-hero for many disaffected young people today, Carole Vopat (1973) claims that the beats ended up reducing the meaning of life to "the Eternal Now, the jazz moment, which demands absolutely nothing" (2004, p. 6). Spontaneity and improvisation offer an ethic, she writes, of *disjunction*, in which young people experience life without limits, liabilities, or obligations. On the road and in their cars, Dean and Sal "are suspended from life and living," she writes. "They seek out not truth nor values but this encapsulated almost fetal existence as an end in itself, and end that is much like death" (Ibid.). The beat concern with freedom she finds to be no more than a freedom from "rational adult life with its welter of consequences and obligations" (Ibid.). Dean is a child, a case of arrested development who justifies his existence not in terms of work or responsibility, but simply in terms of experiencing IT again and again as if IT substitutes for some "lost bliss." Sal acknowledges early on in the novel he and Dean were after "some lost bliss that we probably experience in the womb and can only be reproduced (though we hate to admit it) in death" (Ibid.). This "lost bliss," often achieved with the help of drugs, is clearly part the IT experience for many Phish fans. Mr. Miner, in the blog post cited above, acknowledged that "more addictive than a drug, IT can direct your life if you're not careful." He refers to some obsessive Phish fans who will drive five to eight hours across three states to see a show as "junkies" who just need to "get another fix."

Nathan Rabin (2013) gave a similar account of the addictive quality of IT in *You Don't Know Me But You Don't Like Me*. Rabin finds characters like Dean, for both good and bad, and is drawn to them like Sal. One of them is a young man named Jared, who Rabin re-christens the Golden Child. "Jared had a spirit about him. He had charisma. He had magnetism. His desire to party like no one has ever partied before becomes a strange, glorious, self-fulfilling prophecy" (Rabin, 2013, pp. 125–126). He also had a sexually ambiguous and almost androgenous appeal, so that his best friend can say, "Dude, I fucking love my girlfriend but you have sexy fucking eyes." At the Bethel Woods concert Rabin attends with Jared, "every woman and a number of men smiled at him. With intent" (p. 128). Yet the Golden Child is ultimately more interested in "the possibility if not the promise, of transcendence …[a] spiritual experience," which connects everything in an eternal moment, always ending (p. 126).

The trouble is that the spiritual high for Jared becomes dependent on taking more and more LSD and other drugs to reach the IT space. Rabin reports that the Golden Child almost misses the bus at Bethel Woods because he had taken seven hits of LSD and was found passed out and "lost" or wasted on acid. Jared becomes an archetype for a kind of young man who like Dean in *On the Road*, has "IT," and everyone feeds on his energy and passion for life. Yet he is also, simultaneously a lost child, and arguably losing his way more the longer he stays on the road. Rabin uses "lost" in a dual sense—as being wasted on drugs and aimless—and as in "lost kids" who don't quite fit into conventional society, "flocking to a scene promising a sense of community and solidarity" (p. 22), a space where they will be accepted for who they are and not judged, and where someone will always be there to pick them up when they fall. Rabin himself becomes addicted to the intense spiritual highs and sense of communion with other fans he experiences on the road with Phish, so that even when he trips and splits his head open, he refuses to go to a medical center for stitches because he would have to miss the rest of the concert and desert his friends. His psychiatrist informs him that he may be borderline manic-depressive, and that he is seeking in the manic experience of the Phish concert a way of compensating for his normal depressive state.

The Other Side of Normal

This manic-depressive state may in fact be the "normal" state of people growing up in a society in which the "real" is experienced as drudgery. In such an economic and social order, much work is alienated labor in the classic Marxist sense. People feel detached from the process and the product of their labor and experience work, which in its authentic form is self-enhancing and productive, as mere drudgery. They consequently seek out spaces where they can have ecstatic, fully engaged experiences, where they can "let it all out" in an egalitarian, nonjudgmental, communitarian environment and have spiritual experiences that compensate for what is lacking in their "normal" everyday lives. This lacking is experienced as existential despair. In *On the Road*, Dean experiences despair when he is not on the road and has to support himself and his wife through menial labor, one job after another. For his part, Sal comes home to New York City only to be reminded again of "its millions and millions hustling forever for a buck," of a mad American nightmare of people "grabbing, taking, giving, sighing, dying" (p. 107), buried at last in a drab cemetery in Long Island City. His is tired of life, and feels wretched and miserable, like a ghost "shuddering through nightmare life" (p. 107). The road, to the extent that it is a metaphor for life as a journey, is the only way to live. When you stop too long the despair catches up with you, and so there is really only one way out of this trap for Kerouac: stay on the road and keep moving.

Phish has drawn rather freely from this narrative of being on the road as a way of countering a "normal" life of despair and drudgery. Anastasio has gone so far as to claim in a 2012 interview that the purpose of all that the band does is to give fans a "few moments of happiness" in their lives of "drudgery." But if this is a somewhat serious statement of the band's philosophy, they also have been able to play with the theme of life without Phish as drudgery. The promotional video for Phish's 2013 summer tour, with its *cinema noir* feel, begins with a shot of Fishman peeking out of the venetian blinds in his bleak, cluttered bedroom an exclaiming: "Burlington, Shit. I'm still only in Burlington." He takes another drink and continues, "Every time I think I'm going to wake up on tour." In a deep, raspy, despairing voice he talks about how it used to be worse, that "when I was here I wanted to be there." Now, waiting for the summer tour dates, he says, he is getting "softer, chubbier, clinically obese." Each time he looked around "the walls moved in a little tighter." This is all done in the best tongue-in-cheek style, with Phish poking fun at themselves and their somewhat obsessive fans, deliberately employing the dark narrator's voice of the down-and-out detective wasting away in his office or hotel room until the phone rings and a new client draws him back into life on a great adventure. Similarly, going on tour draws that band and its fans back to life and gets them out of their world-weariness. Anastasio's comments suggest that this narrative is not all tongue-in-cheek, that people need to go on the road periodically to break out of the drudgery that comes with staying at home, with the familiar, routine pattern of everyday life and work.

Beat Culture

This is clearly the only option for Dean, being on the road in pursuit of IT or at home sinking into despair. Kerouac seems to be suggesting that this is pretty well what people are stuck with so long as they follow only the *Tathagata* path of non-attachment in pursuit of bliss. As I said earlier, the other path to enlightenment that interested Kerouac was that of *Bodhisattva*, of acting to alleviate human suffering and fight against injustices and the degradation of life and nature. This still requires a return to the real and the moment, but in a way that moves beyond the pursuit of personal bliss alone. Kerouac, and his character Sal, moves in this direction through the writing of a novel based on three long road trips. *On the Road* is an intervention on the side of the common folk, celebrating their common wisdom and empathizing with their plights. Kerouac is often accused, and justifiably so, of a patronizing depiction of African Americans and Mexican Americans as exotic Others more in touch with their primal selves than uptight, middle class, White Americans. But this meant he also looked to them as more enlightened, as having something that might help save America. When Dean is passed out on a Mexican highway beside his car, where Sal sleeps, a policeman comes over to check on them to see that they are okay, without suspicion, that he viewed himself as the "guardian of the sleeping town" (p. 242)—completely different from what they would expect in the U.S. where policemen might have beaten or arrested them, where everyone was always under suspicion until proven innocent, especially if you were down on your luck. Sal and Dean's identification with Black and Latino bebop music, and the non-White space of the Black and Latino jazz club, was itself a radical act in the late 1940s, and it signaled a new willingness among some White youth to build alliances across the great racial and ethnic divides of their day. Bebop jazz was not just about recovering a lost bliss. It also was a blowing of outrage at all the forces that beat people of color down and kept them in their place.

I am reminded of a passage from James Baldwin's great novel, *Another Country* (1962), describing a member of a bebop band in 1950s Harlem who "blows" his outrage:

> He was a kid.. from some insane place like Jersey City or Syracuse, but somewhere along the line he had discovered that he could say it with a saxophone ..... They were being assaulted by the saxophonist who perhaps no longer wanted their love and merely hurled his outrage at them with the same contemptuous, pagan pride with which he humped the air .... Each man knew that the boy was blowing for every one of them. (p. 6).

In Baldwin's character, "blowing" functions to express his outrage as a young Black man growing up on the mean streets of America's urban landscape, without opportunity, beat down, but no longer just beat down, now blowing back and holding nothing back. Unlike an older generation of Black Americans in the North who had sought to go unnoticed, since being noticed by Whites often meant being beat down, the bebop generation would blow its outrage and affirm that (to paraphrase a Queer Nation chant), we're here, we're Black, and get used to it. To blow was a political act, of defiance, outrage, and creative self-production all simultaneously. White middle class youth could not fully relate to the outrage of their Black and Brown brothers and sisters since they had not lived with racism. But they could relate to the blowing of outrage, against the lost promise of what America could have been and should have been, and outrage all the "masters" of the world who beat people down and seek to keep them under their thumb, so to speak. In Phish culture, the archetypal "master" is represented by "Wilson," the despotic ruler in Phish's founding mythology of "Gamehendge." When Phish perform the song "Wilson," fans chant "Wilson" at appropriate spots, raising their fists in the air in a collective act of outrage and defiance at all the Wilsons they have known in their lives and that they pledge to do battle against.

Bebop and beat culture obviously had a progressive cultural politics, from its critique of an America that seemed to have lost its way in the celebration of wealth, status, materialism, and shallowness. It also actively began to construct a counter-space within the dominant culture where young people lived according to different values—arguably more democratic, egalitarian, and accepting of difference. Unlike the generation that followed in the 1960s and that would resurrect idealism and hope in the face of despair, the beats were less able to see a way out of the materialistic mindlessness, mind-numbing conformity and Cold War madness of the late 1940s and early 1950s in the U.S. One might say that the current generation of young people is in a similar spot, and that their music might be called the new realism, about grabbing a few moments of bliss in a life of drudgery, building an "underground" culture as a place to occasionally escape. If that is so, we have much to learn by going back to the beats and bebop culture, to reveal both its progressive promise and its contradictions and limits.

Sal and Dean find wild bebop bars and clubs everywhere they go across the U.S. and in Mexico, with local and traveling bands blowing long into the night. So already by the late 1940s, bebop music and youth culture was a national and even international phenomenon, no longer limited to the boroughs of New York City and their ethnic street gangs. Now there would be an alternative to a "life adjustment" education of the late 1940s, and America would never be the same again. Bebop may have had nothing to say lyric-wise, but it had everything to say as a sensibility, an attitude, a lifestyle, an identity, and a counterculture. That counterculture educated young people as hip, evolving, open, creative, improvisational, empowered subjects, but also as subjects who embraced life in the face of despair, as an active choice. In this they reflected the existential philosophy of the age, which taught people how to make meaning in their lives and find purpose in a universe without any prior meaning and in which suffering and death is our inevitable fate.

There is a rather direct genealogy that connects this beat attitude with Phish culture. The song *Haley's Comet* contains this oft-quoted line among Phish fans: "What is the central theme of this elaborate spoof?" Given that life is a "spoof," an absurdity in the end, what is its purpose. One answer provided by Kerouac and Phish is that the meaning to this elaborate spoof is only to be found by returning to "IT," to the moment and the emerging field of action in which we always finding ourselves, connected to other people and the material world, and always affirming life and consequently meaning in the face of despair and alienation. Neither Kerouac nor Phish would seek to shelter young people from the dark side of life, from the abyss we all have to confront and walk away from, choosing life over the void. A Phish song titled *Rift* is about someone approaching "a rift, an edge of a cliff, beneath which lies the abyss, a darkness the light from above could not reach." On this edge, the person does battle with his own destiny—which is to die and ultimately be defeated. As his destiny slips over the edge, it "shocked and persuaded my soul to ignite," shocking him back life and re-igniting his passion for living here and now, without a destiny other than one he chooses for himself.

Conclusion

Kerouac (like Phish) looked to bebop and the IT experience as a kind of shock treatment in the face of despair, causing the "soul to ignite" and perhaps, with enough sparks, ignite a cultural transformation in America. He also suggests that IT only happens when people break out of their normal routine, in which they perceive life as only drudgery and boredom, and go on the road—metaphorically if not literally. In the novel, Dean asks Sal: "What's your road, man?—holyboy road, madman road, rainbow road, guppy road, any road. It's an anywhere road for anybody anyhow" (p. 251). As Hilary Holaday (2008) notes, "Kerouac's readers, even his detractors, have always understood that the road trip stands for the life trip" (p. ix). It expressed, in the post-WWII era, a restlessness, a need to get up and follow a dream, to experience new and different cultures, to break away if only briefly from the mind-numbing drudgery and routine of young people's lives, to reconnect with friends and find community on the road, and to have an ecstatic spiritual experience along the way. Dean implies that what you make of the road trip is very much dependent on your attitude and perspectives. A "holyboy" road understands experiences along the road in terms of the forces of good versus those of evil, and of the need to stay true to the good, the virtuous, the moral life. The "madman" experiences the world of the road from the perspective of an outsider in a society of docile, "normal," pacified citizens and consumers. The madman knows, as the *Fool on the Hill* knew in the Beatles song of that name, that they're the fools, they're the madmen and women, and that changes everything. It breaks through the commonsense of the dominant culture and thus creates a rupture in culture, a break, a tear, that would only grow wider and deeper in the years that followed. Bebop and the beats constructed a democratic progressive youth culture based on rebellion and defiance of growing up to be "normal," docile citizens and workers—whether in the U.S.S.R. or the U.S.A. This was a model of social change based on the rebellion of the young against all established orders, disciplinary powers, and "schooling" as a form of miseducation. Bebop and beat culture thus established a dialectic between youth culture and adult culture, in which youth assumed an active and even leading role in the dialectic, and this meant they had to come up with their own answers, and they had to pursue their own destinies, on the road of life.

References

Adorno, T. (2001). *The culture industry: Selected essays on mass culture*. New York: Routledge.
Dittman, M. J. (2004). *Jack Kerouac a biography*. Westport, CT: Greenwood Press.
Dittman, M. J. (2007). *Masterpieces of beat literature*. Westport, CT: Greenwood Press.
Gattghan, F. (2004). Kerouac, Jack. In Michael Kimmel & Amy Aronson (Eds.), *Men and masculinities: A social, cultural, and historical encyclopedia* (pp. 452–453). Santa Barbara, CA: ABS-CLEO.
Gillespie, D. (2009). *To be or not … to bop*. Minneapolis: University of Minnesota Press.
Ginsberg, A. (1993). The visions of the great remember. In Jack Kerouac (Ed.), *Visions of Cody*. New York: Penguin Books.
Goodman, P. (1960). *Growing up absurd: Problems of youth in the Organized Society*. New York: Vintage Books.
Haddix, C. (2013). *Bird: The life and music of Charlie Parker*. Champaign: University of Illinois Press.
Holaday, H. (2008). *What's your road man? Critical essays on Jack Kerouac's on the road*. Carbondale: Southern Illinois University Press.
Keroac, J. (1957). *On the road*. New York: Viking Press.
Kun, J. (2005). *Audiotopia: Music, race, and America*. Berkeley: University of California Press.
McRae, B. (1989). *Dizzy Gillespie: His life and times*. London, UK: Omnibus Press.
Puterbaugh, P. (2009). *Phish: The biography*. Cambridge, MA: Da Capo Press.
Rabin, N. (2013). *You don't know me but you don't like me*. New York: Scribner.
Schneider, E. C. (2001). *Vampires, dragons, and Egyptian kings: Youth gangs in postwar New York*. Princeton, NJ: Princeton University Press.
Shipton, A. (1999). *Groovin' high: The life of Dizzy Gillespie*. New York: Oxford University Press.

Theado, M. (2000). *Understanding Jack Kerouac*. Columbia: University of South Carolina Press.
Vopat, C. (2004). Jack Kerouac's *on the road*: A re-evaluation. In Harold Bloom (Ed.), *Jack Kerouac's On The Road*. Broomall, PA: Chelsea House Publishers.
Vopat, C. G. (2000). Jack Kerouac's *On the road*: A re-evaluation. In Marie Rose Napierkowski & Deborah Stanley, et al. (Eds.), *Midwest quarterly 14 (summer 1973): 385–407. Rpt. in novels for students* (Vol. 8, pp. 195–201). Detroit, MI: Gale. Print.
Watson, S. (1998). *The birth of the beat generation: Visionaries, rebels, and hipsters, 1944–1960*. New York: Pantheon Books.

Chapter Two

Phishy Folk

Trey Unplugged

When Trey Anastasio performed Phish songs with an acoustic guitar at the Newport Folk Festival in 2008, he symbolically connected Phish (still in hiatus at that time) to the folk revival of the 1950s and 1960s in the U.S. and to the moment the revival began to collapse in 1965. In a seminal performance that epitomized this denouement at the Newport Folk Festival that year, Bob Dylan (who had performed acoustic there the previous two years and become the young face and hope of the folk revival) "plugged-in." In this venue where everyone else was performing acoustic, he performed rock. In a parody through reversal of this earlier moment, Anastasio, known for his electric guitar and extended guitar jamming, went acoustic and thus traditional at a festival in which most "folk" performers were plugged-in and blurring the lines between folk, rock, country, and the blues. This was a way of paying homage to folk music as a living legacy, one that has played an important role in connecting young people to movements for social change organized around equity, social justice, freedom, and the building of inclusive communities of difference and diversity. At the same time, by playing with the memory of Dylan's appearance in 1965, and its subversive quality, Anastasio was affirming that artists and musicians should not try to live up to other's expectations for them—even their legions of young fans. Some Phish fans were disappointed to see Anastasio go acoustic at the Newport Folk Festival, just like some of Dylan's fans were disappointed when he plugged-in at Newport. Jon Fishman of Phish has remarked, "I really admire musicians like Miles Davis and Bob Dylan, because they completely ignored the critics and naysayers and forged ahead with a music they truly believed in." When he was booed by folk purists, he never let it bother him too much. "His strength of conviction," according to Fishman, "is what makes him a great artist."

Phish has not included many folk artists or songs from the folk revival in their repertoire, but they have acknowledged some influential songs arranged and performed by Pete Seeger, the towering figure who almost willed the movement into existence from its beginnings until its end. Phish.net acknowledges Phish covers of three Seeger songs are from the 1950s. Two of these songs are from 1951 when Seeger was performing with the popular Decca recording group, the Weavers—namely, *Wimoweh* (later re-named in *The Lion Sleeps Tonight* when it was recorded by the Tokens in 1961), and *The Banks Are Made of Marble*—one of the Weavers non-commercial, political songs. The Seeger song performed most often, *Living in the Country*, is from the late 1950s. Each of these songs is a well-known Seeger song, and each represents a different aspect of the folk revival. Consequently, their selection says something about a Phish folk sensibility, a certain non-commercialism and anti-"boss" politics, a commitment to equity and diversity, a relationship between performers and their audiences that is dialectic rather than one-way, and a commitment to the specificity of the performance of music at outdoor festival venues.

Nevertheless, these Phish connections to Seeger and the folk revival are nominally noteworthy, as if they were thrown in as a musical wink and a nod to a folk revival that in actuality held little influence over them. Phish has only covered *The Lion Sleeps Tonight* once; and the other two songs were performed by Mike Gordon when he was touring with

Leo Kottke, so they do not actually qualify as Phish covers despite the fact they are listed under Seeger covers in Phish.net. The most overtly political of these songs, *The Banks Are Made of Marble*, was performed by Gordon and Kottke only twice, in late 2002 when they were touring together. They also performed *Living in the Country* 16 times during that tour. It is likely Kottke, somewhat of a folk purist, suggested these songs since they were in his concert repertoire, and he is sometimes even mistakenly credited with writing the songs although he always gives credit to Seeger. The fact that this is the extent of Phish's venturing into the muddy waters of the folk revival speaks to the cultural rupture or divide that has separated folk revival music, on the one hand, and both bebop jazz and the beats, and the progressive rock movement that Dylan presaged in 1965, on the other. Yet this presumed divide needs to be troubled, something Gordon in his appearances with Kottke, Anastasio at the Newport Folk Festival, and Phish in their performance of *The Lion Sleeps Tonight* have sought to do, and they have done it in a way that pays tribute to both Pete Seeger and Dylan.

Pete Seeger and Phish

Born into a wealthy upstate New York family of German ancestry, Seeger always had the privilege of choosing a life, free of concerns about making a living. His father was a music professor at UC-Berkeley—a life he too had the privilege of choosing—at least until he was fired for opposing the U.S. entry into World War I. It is not altogether unheard of that the wealthy, born into wealth and feeling drawn to the plight of the poor and the downtrodden, wish they could help in some way; and they do, although always from a position of privilege, and armed with an elite ideology of uplifting the poor and those less privileged than themselves. Pete Seeger was only able to transcend some of this privilege while he was with the common folk, as when he traveled with Woody Guthrie, although perhaps he was also inescapably performing the "gentleman-adventurer" role then as well. His leftist politics at least provided a coherent way of recognizing and critiquing his own privilege by subordinating himself to the needs of the people, the party, and the cause. As a young boy, Seeger had already come across *New Russia's Primer* in the school library, and was influenced by its message to young people, to watch for decadent tendencies in their own behavior, and that of their friends, parents, and even teachers. The Young Pioneer movement in Soviet Russia, a kind of communist boy scouts, expressed both the idealism of the revolution and the need for discipline, ideological purity, and action that Seeger embraced at an impressionable age and that stayed with him, in modified and less doctrinaire form, throughout the next decades. As a boy he watched squads of young volunteers from Communist Party unemployment councils fan out into the Lower East Side, helping evicted tenants find shelter, food, clothing, and other services. But he was equally influenced it seems by Ernest Thompson Seton's Woodcraft League, a variation on the "muscular Christianity" movement that promoted physical fitness, hygiene, and moral rigor (abstinence) for adolescent males. One might imagine that Seeger, educated in this context of religious Calvinism and a rather orthodox version of Communism, would find in folk music (like the party and progressive elements in the church) something to like, something that seemed to fit his temper and his sense of purpose.

Seeger had been introduced to folk music by his father, who even arranged a meeting with the famous Delta Blues songwriter and performer, Leadbelly, whose version of *House of the Rising Sun* would become a rock standard covered by the Animals in the 1960s. After dropping out of Harvard feeling he was wasting his time, that he could better educate himself, Seeger began working better, he began working for Alan Lomax, director of the folk music collection at the Library of Congress and a major figure in the folk movement. There, in 1942, he joined a commune of other folk artists, including Woody Guthrie, who formed the Almanac Singers—a group committed to singing songs in support of labor unions and racial justice. In 1945 he helped organize People's Songs, dedicated to the dissemination of progressive folk music, and in 1948, when Henry Wallace of the Progressive Party ran for president, folk singers from People's Songs played a significant role in his campaign as part of a larger Popular Front of musicians and artists. By the late 1940s, the Almanac Singers had morphed into the Weavers, and by 1951 they were among the top pop groups in the country, consistently having records on the "Hit Parade" for several months at a time.

One of their biggest hits was *Wimoweh*, released as a 78 RPM record by Decca in 1951, an example of an effort by the Weavers to bring ethnic music from around the globe to American young people in the interests of promoting world peace and an early form of global multiculturalism. *Wimoweh* was originally a Zulu song from South Africa, prominently features Seeger's mispronounced lyric of the song's original chorus, *Uyimbube*, which in Zulu translates as, "You are a lion" (Seeger, 1993, p. 90). In Seeger's description of the song in *Where Have All the Flowers Gone* (1993), he goes out of his way to make the anti-Apartheid politics of the song overt and lays out some of what is referenced in the song. "The lion" (ibid.) is Zulu Chaka, the last great Zulu king before colonial domination began in the 19th century. "When he died," Seeger wrote, "the legend arose that the Lion was not dead; he was only sleeping, and would someday wake up." In the original South African recording of the song, Solomon Linda calls out to young, Black South Africans, "You are the lion! You are the lion!": But South African songs of freedom under the Apartheid regime, like African American spirituals under slavery and Jim Crow, had to be carefully coded so that their political meaning could be denied and even go unheard by most listeners. Seeger recounts a conversation with a producer from Gallo Records, the South African company that had recorded Solomon Linda for a South African audience of young people. Seeger asked the man what the Zulu name of the song meant. "The lion is sleeping, the lion, the lion." Then Seeger wanted to know whether Africans ever attempt to put political words in their songs. To which the man replied, "Oh, they try it all the time, but we weed it out." To Seeger, this deliberate de-politicization of popular music was not just demanded in Apartheid South Africa, it was demanded in the U.S. as well. The de-politicization of the song "Wimoweh" was facilitated by the fact that it had no lyrics as such, only the one word "Wimoweh" chant. That meant it really needed a narrative introduction, as Seeger has since provided in his own reflections on the song. But the song was performed without an introduction in the Decca 78 RPM recording, so the young fans of the Weavers were buying an upbeat, rhythmic song essentially stripped of context. When it was finally released in the album, *The Weavers: 1949–1953*, Seeger does begin the song with a brief discussion of the Zulu origins of the song and that the key to its meaning is in "that one word in the Zulu language. A missionary told us it means a lion, whatever that means." Here we see Seeger deliberately participating in promoting a very non-political interpretation of the song, invoking the knowledge of a White missionary regarding its meaning. At the same time, he teases the listener with the idea that a lion may not be a lion, that is, that it may mean something symbolic. In recent years, Seeger has acknowledged that he did some things wrong in the recording of "Wimoweh." He did not pronounce Zulu words correctly and omitted completely Solomon Linda's call to the audience, "You are the lion!" At least, he says in his defense, he did not do to the song what the Tokens did with their 1961 hit, "The Lion Sleeps Tonight." That group created totally new lyrics for the song, located it in a jungle when there are no jungles in South Africa, and changed the title. For Seeger, "this trivializes a song of great historical importance." The trivialization continued when Disney Studios re-made the Token's version of the song for *The Lion King* (1994).

Within the context of a growing resistance to Apartheid both within South Africa and around the world, "Wimoweh" was an anti-colonial political anthem of freedom to those who understood its deeper meaning. Yet, when the popular recording of the song was released by Decca, without filling in this context, it hardly seemed political at all, merely a simple tribal song about the village being safe at night because the lion is sleeping accompanied by an upbeat rhythm and an a cappella, do wop-like chorus. Is a song subversive politically if it is not heard as such, if it is sold as a mass-produced commodity, like cigarettes? That was a question that began to haunt Seeger after the Weavers struck it big with songs like "Wimoweh."

That is a question that can also be asked of Phish's performance of the song, on February 18, 2003, in Denver, Colorado. In the evening's second set, a jam of *You Enjoy Myself* (YEM) resolved into *The Lion Sleeps Tonight* to end the show. Many fans, according to Phish.net, were disappointed that the band did not close with YEM since it was a popular song to end on. If the fans in attendance knew *The Lion Sleeps*

Tonight, it was probably because they had heard the Tokens' recording. While the Phish.net post does acknowledge that the song was first a hit in Swaziland and that Seeger and the Weavers recorded it as *Wimoweh*, the post concludes that it is a "song about hunting a sleeping lion." It is clear that the band members trace the song back to Seeger and the Weavers and across the decades, but stripped of its cultural context, it has lost almost all political meaning. That was no doubt how it was received by Phish fans in 2003. Many would have been familiar with the Disney animated classic *The Lion King* and probably assumed the song was written for the movie.

While it is possible, even easy, to de-politicize the overt cultural politics encoded in a song like *Wimoweh*, and to strip it from its historical and cultural context, the same cannot be said for another song recorded by Seeger and the Weavers in 1951—*The Banks Are Made of Marble*—that has been performed twice by Mike Gordon of Phish with Leo Kottke, in two consecutive nights in November 2002, while they were on tour together. Since the song had been part of Kottke's repertoire, it seems likely he was the one who brought this piece to Gordon's attention and suggested they perform it together. The song was written between 1948 and 1949 by Les Rice, an apple farmer in upstate New York whose songs were known throughout the northeast among farm union organizers and activists. In a note in one of his songbooks, Seeger wrote that "like most small farmers, he [Rice] was getting intolerably squeezed by the big companies which sold him all his fertilizer, insecticide and equipment ..." The song describes banks, with guards at every door, as vaults "stuffed with silver/That the farmer sweated for." It ends with a call to action: "I've seen my brothers working .../I prayed we'd get together/and together make a stand." Seeger and the Weavers understood that the overt, anti-big business lyrics of the song would make it unacceptable as a mainstream Decca release; so they did not even pursue that possibility. Seeger recalls, "We just knew that there was no point to it—they wouldn't record those songs." The group proceeded to record the song on a small label and it was largely overlooked by radios, music stores, and fans of the group but would have an enormous influence within the Popular Front and among farmer unions.

The song would not go unnoticed either by Senator McCarthy and the House Un-American Activity Committee (HUAC), which was investigating the influence of communists and communist sympathizers in the government and in the entertainment and news industries. The Communist Party's Popular Front and groups like the Weavers who identified with it were under suspicion and beginning to be brought before the house committee, which had the power to destroy their careers by "black-listing" them. Ironically, this was happening at a time when the Weavers seemed to be in the process of going commercial, no longer a threat to the cultural orthodoxy and rabid anti-communism that gripped the nation. In this summer of 1952, the Weavers recordings of *Kisses Sweeter Than Wine* and *So Long, It's Been Good to Know You* were climbing the hit parade charts, and Seeger began to feel that his singing partners—under pressure from Decca—had decided to become pop stars and leave their political music days behind. In the documentary film about Seeger, *The Power of Song* (2007), he observes that he finally felt compelled to resign from the Weavers when the three other band members agreed to perform in a cigarette commercial.

All of this mainstreaming of the Weavers, and Seeger's increasing frustration with the mainstreaming of the Weavers, ironically was occurring at the same time that the FBI and the HUAC were investigating them. An FBI informant, later convicted of perjury, swore before the committee that members of the Weavers were Communist Party members. That effectively ended the commercial viability of the Weavers, and their record company (Decca) dropped them. But it was just the beginning of the black-listing and harassment of Seeger by HUAC. In August 1955, he was called before the committee, where he refused to answer questions regarding his political beliefs, stating instead, "these are very improper questions for any American to be asked." Congress charged him with contempt and he fought off and on with the committee through the end of the 1950s as his black-listing by major record labels and network television companies continued.

The early folk revival, up through the early 1950s, had been based on a leftist progressive conviction that folk music could educate the masses in their own diverse folk heritages, as living legacies that can be used to reach the common folk with new, revised messages. Folk music was to be the curriculum and the pedagogy of social reconstructionism, grounded in a view of the working class, or the common folk, as the makers of the revolution, with folk musicians and artists assigned the role of the public intellectual, assuming a role that public schools could not or would not serve. Woody Guthrie, along with Pete Seeger, lived and breathed that role and made a life out of it. But the folk revival of the mid-1940s through early 1950s was plagued by contradictions and dilemmas and undermined its capacity to assume such a socially reconstructive educational role. First, by the late 1940s, the "Old Left" that had spawned the first folk revival was under attack from the political right, in the form of the McCarthy hearings, but also from a growing number of progressives in the U.S. concerned about the political dogmatism and conformity of Soviet communism. The Old Left proved unable to reinvent itself in a new age, and it would be another decade before a younger generation would reconstitute the left as the New Left, out of which the second folk revival would be born. As Todd Gitlin maintains, the early folk revival was a "defunct movement," only "holding the place of a Left in American culture" that was more nostalgic and imaginary than real, more organically connected to middle-class college students than to the real working class or marginalized groups.

Second, in the face of rising pressure from their record company, Decca, the Weavers (with Seeger's disapproval) began to turn out a string of "Hit Parade" hits, with no obvious cultural politics other than the celebration of conventional family values and moral virtue. The overt cultural politics of early Popular Front songs like *The Banks Are Made of Marble* was replaced by a rather nostalgic populist politics, in which moral rigor and positive values are preached to the masses, as in the group's most popular hit, *Goodnight Irene*. One thing this means, I think, is that authentic music artists always have a tenuous relationship with the pop music industry, and that top 40 music—like that produced by the Weavers in the early 1950s—crosses over a certain line in which music becomes commodified, produced and assembled on an assembly line of recorded sound, with the artist a worker (even if a well-paid one) estranged from the final product—as Seeger finally was.

The Weavers banishment from the world of pop music and the pursuit of a mass audience would, in that sense, be a godsend.

Finally, the music of the early folk revival, in its most popular forms, taught moral virtue to young people that failed to connect with a rising tide of discontent among American youth. The Soviets were bringing up a generation of well-behaved, model communist citizens both in their public schools and through the production of revolutionary "folk" music and the censoring of "decadent" Western rock n' roll. And in the U.S., both public schools and popular "folk" music, like that performed by the Weavers fulfilled much the same role. It is hardly surprising that folk music in its populist form came into the school music curriculum very quickly, so that young people in by the mid-1950s were learning to sing songs by the Weavers along with Woody Guthrie in their music classes. They taught "wholesome" values, and virtues related to the "public good." This is, in retrospect, a curriculum that seeks to normalize young people, in some good ways but ultimately in ways that were over-conforming and would be resisted by a growing number of young people who began to defy the clean-cut norms set for them by a parental generation and looked elsewhere for music of resistance and agency.

When Seeger arranged and recorded *Living in the Country* in 1959 and 1960, his political and social resurrection was almost complete, and he was the acknowledged leader of a new folk revival, organized around and through the Newport Folk Festival, which he helped found in 1959. His politics had shifted from the early 1950s as he continued to distance himself from a Communist Party and a Soviet Union that was clearly bankrupt and had little to offer democratic progressives in America. He, like many "progressives" (although that term too fell out of favor) mobilized around the global peace and anti-nuke movement, the Civil Rights Movement of African Americans in the Jim Crow South, and an incipient environmental movement against unrestricted economic development and degradation of the earth. Soon the global peace movement would link-up with a growing anti-Vietnam war movement among American youth. Many of the songs of the second folk revival, from the late 1950s through the mid-1960s, were overtly political, like Seeger's *Where Have All the Flowers Gone*, and his revival and re-working of the African American spiritual, *We Shall Overcome*, which became the unofficial anthem of the Civil Rights Movement.

But Seeger also liked to revive and re-work folk "originals" without an overt political message, and one of the most popular of these is *Living in the Country*. He wrote that the song was sung by African American dockworkers on the coast of Georgia early in the 20th century, with a chorus that included, "Pay me. Oh pay me, pay me my money down" (Seeger, 1993, p. 77). But Seeger noted that this "original" was actually an African American re-working of a 19th century English sea chant, *Blow the Man Down*. Seeger's own version, which he described as "a new piece of music," sounded more like bluegrass than anything else, but was meant to represent multicultural diversity. The folk revival was not, in spite of the claims of some, a "purist" movement in which songs had to be performed as much like the "original" as possible. Quite the contrary, folk artists like Seeger and others, always created something new and this was at least partially because they recognized the original did not exist and could not be recovered, that re-working a song was the highest form of flattery.

There is something particularly progressive about not being a purist, so long as the line is not crossed that separates authentic art from highly-commercialized music written and produced only to make a lot of money and so long as you give credit where credit is due. Seeger wrote lyrics for *Living in the Country* which presents a brief history of the guitar, from the gypsies in Europe, to the Spanish, to Mexicans, to African Americans, who learned to play it like a drum band. This is Seeger as the teacher again, giving young people a lesson on how multicultural and diverse American cultural heritages are, and how inseparably interlocked and interrelated they all are. Americans who play a guitar today are connected to all of these histories of usage and performance, whether they know it or not. Without these lyrics and this genealogy, the song is typically performed today as a Seeger standard, or as a Kottke standard, and that is the way Kottke and Gordon performed it when they were on tour together.

Seeger performed *Living in the Country* at the Newport Folk Festival in the early 1960s, at a time when the festival and the folk revival was at its height and was attracting growing attention among a generation of college students who were more idealistic than their predecessors, more invested in the idea that they could make a difference, and that folk music could make a difference. The festival had been organized and held for the first time in 1959, as a business venture but with its board members—including Seeger, Theodore Bikel, Oscar Brand, and Albert Grossman—committed to providing a space for established and aspiring folk artists to perform, without concern for the music's commercial viability, and with a deliberate effort made to represent a diversity of American folk music traditions. The artists and songs featured on the poster for the first festival included Pete Seeger performing *Careless Love*, a song of moral virtue from the Weavers' era; Joan Baez performing *Crossing the Jordan River*, a gospel song identified with the civil rights movement; Sonny Terry and Brownie McGhee performing *My Baby Done Changed the Lock on the Door*, a Delta blues song sung from the perspective of a beat down Black man; Earl Scruggs performing *Cumberland Gap*, representing White bluegrass and country-folk music; and Odetta performing *Cotton Fields At Home*, an African American country blues standard. From the beginning, the board of directors wanted to make it clear that the new folk revival would be more diverse and less doctrinaire than the first one, and that the festival would welcome commercially successful, clean-cut, collegiate groups like the Kingston Trio (who performed much of the old Weavers repertoire), along with more authentic folk artists who were less commercially successful. By 1965, under the leadership of Seeger, the festival changed to a not-for-profit organization supported by a foundation. A growing number of young people inspired by President Kennedy's idealism had found in folk revival music a vehicle for the expression of their rage at injustices, and for the promotion of their idealistic hopes and dreams that democracy in America might begin to live up its promise if we all speak up and take a stand to demand change. But the movement continued to be ignored by many young people who saw it as too wholesome and too "*Kum Ba Yah*." The young folk revival fans at the Newport Folk Festival sat or stood quietly while the artists performed with only a small microphone to amplify the sound. You had to be attentive, quiet, and serious. There was no room for defiant language, loud, amplified music, and youthful resistance to parental authority figures—all the things that rock music, as a British and American fusion—was beginning to offer the "Boomer" generation by 1965.

Dylan must have known the time was right, that it was (as he would say) his destiny to be the one who fused folk music with the power and rebelliousness of rock—the new music of the counterculture, which was after all a contemporary music form created by fusing folk, blues and bluegrass/country music. When Dylan "plugged-in" at Newport, he was not being as subversive of the folk revival as purists claimed he was. He was just taking the folk revival to its next logical phase, not rejecting folk music, only rejecting the purist, tradition-bound mentality within the folk revival. He had, early on, been a purist himself, singing the songs of Woody Guthrie and emulating his style, even his look. Even after he began to write his own songs, connecting them to contemporary civil rights struggles, he adhered to the folk revival norm of acoustic-only performances before quiet and attentive folk music fans, and revered Seeger almost like a father—a feeling that apparently was reciprocated. Dylan's first appearance at the Newport Folk Festival was in 1963, when he was introduced by Joan Baez but already acknowledged as the *Wunderkind* of the movement. For the festival finale, he brought to the stage Baez, the Student Nonviolent Coordinating Committee's (SNCC) Freedom Singers (including Bernice Johnson), and Peter, Paul, and Mary, to sing *Blowin' in the Wind*; then closed the entire festival by bringing a few more voices to the stage, including Seeger and Theodore Bikel, for a rousing, hand-clapping rendition of *We Shall Overcome*. That was "the apogee of the folk movement," Bikel later said. "There was no point more suffused with hope for the future" (Bikel cited in Dunaway, 2008, p. 280).

By the summer of 1965, however, times were changing again, nationally and for Dylan. The idealism that President Kennedy had embodied for a young generation of Americans, and the belief that everyone individually and collectively could make a difference, was expressed in the Peace Corps, for example, and its ethic of service and helping build bridges between different cultures, and the singing of folk songs like *We Shall Overcome* during Peace Corps training helped volunteers build bonds of solidarity and gave them a sense of purpose that was linked symbolically to the Civil Rights movement. This idealism was also expressed during Freedom Summer in 1964 in which Black and White college students brought together by the Student Nonviolent Coordinating Committee (SNCC) in Oxford, Ohio, sang folk songs as part of their preparation for their bus trip to register Black voters in the South—from which three would not return. By the summer of 1965, young people and the nation were a bit less idealistic, recognizing that the battles against racism and poverty would go on, that the North had its own problems, and that funding for President Johnson's newly-declared "War on Poverty" was being diverted into the sink-hole of Vietnam, and it was lining the pockets of those at the top of a vast "military-industrial complex." Meanwhile, something new was emerging in youth culture in San Francisco.

In the summer of 1964, Ken Kesey and the Merry Pranksters had taken their hippie bus "Furthur" across the country conducting "acid tests" along the way, and in New York City the Velvet Underground was beginning to perform in Greenwich Village, combining beat generation influences in their lyrics and philosophy of life with complex rock arrangements. Dylan was aware of, and seemed to reflect, these subtle shifts that were occurring in middle-class youth culture, and his music was evolving with them. He became, more about breaking free of the constraints of mainstream society, finding a space to work and live outside the madness that was descending upon the nation, more about consciousness-raising and spiritual rebirth. These were beat generation themes and reflect the fact that Allan Ginsberg rather than Seeger was beginning to influence his politics.

On the evening Dylan was to perform, Seeger sat backstage, unaware that Dylan's crew was setting up huge amplifiers on stage. Dylan appeared not in his usual working-class outfit—his Woody Guthrie look—but rather in a black leather jacket, black slacks, pointed motorcycle boots, and a yellow dress shirt, with dark glasses covering his eyes from view. With Al Kooper and the Paul Butterfield Blues Band backing him up, Dylan began playing *Maggie's Farm* on an electric Fender guitar, and when he felt it was not loud enough, he called out "louder" to the sound man. A riveting blues number, *Maggie's Farm* was a political song if it was heard that way. It could be taken to mean that Dylan was not going to work for the military-industrial complex, no longer work on the farm of capitalism or "God and Law." It is not a song, however, about taking over *Maggie's Farm*, only no longer working on one, and trying to carve out a counter-space somewhere outside the mainstream.

What happened when Dylan performed *Maggie's Farm* plugged-in, is the stuff of myth, by which I mean that a few facts have been weaved together to tell a particular narrative about a child (Dylan) challenging the Oedipal father (Seeger), a younger generation taking leadership from a parental one. Seeger has supported the general facts: that he was angry with Dylan for playing electric, and so loudly that he could not hear the words, and that he threatened to cut the cable to the amplifier. That year, the Newport Folk Festival board of directors, with the strong opposition of Seeger, had decided to permit "electric" instruments in the festival, and this must have seemed the ultimate outcome to Seeger.

Conclusion

While the Civil Rights movement continued with an increasing emphasis on racism in the North, and on economic inequality, some of the purity and idealism of the early Civil Rights movement was missing. With Kennedy's assassination, the idealistic Peace Corps mentality promoted among the nation's youth began to be tempered a bit, and college students were drawn increasingly to consciousness-raising, and to finding a place of freedom within a "system" and set of institutions that seemingly would always be corrupt, unjust, and authoritarian.

References

Cantwell, R. (1996). *When we were good: The folk revival*. Cambridge, MA: Harvard University Press.
Cohen, R. D. (1995). *"Wasn't that a time!": Firsthand accounts of the folk music revival*. Metuchen, NJ: Scarecrow Press.
Cohen, R. D. (2002). *Rainbow quest: The folk music revival and American society, 1940–1970*. Amherst: University of Massachusetts Press.
Cohen, R. D. (2006). *Folk music: The basics*. New York, NY: Routledge.

Cohen, R. D. (2008). *A history of folk music festivals in the United States: Feasts of musical celebration*. Lanham, MD: Scarecrow Press.

Cohen, R. D., & Samuelson, D. (1996). *Songs for political action*. Hambergen, Germany: Bear Family Records.

Common Dreams. (2011). *A song by Les Rice: The banks are made of marble*. Retrieved from: https://www.commondreams.org/view/2011/10/22-0

De Turk, D., & Poulin, A. Jr. (1967). *The American folk scene: Dimensions of the folksong revival*. New York, NY: Dell.

Denisoff, R. S. (1971). *Great day coming: Folk music and the American left*. Urbana: University of Illinois Press.

Denisoff, R. S. (1972). *Sing a song of social significance*. Bowling Green, OH: Bowling Green University Popular Press.

Donaldson, R. C. (2014). *"I hear America singing": Folk music and national identity*. Philadelphia, PA: Temple University Press.

Dunaway, D. K. (2008). *How can I keep from singing?: The ballad of Pete Seeger*. New York, NY: Villard.

Eyerman, R., & Barretta, S. (1996). From the 30s to the 60s: The folk Music Revival in the United States. *Theory and Society, 25*, 501–543.

Eyerman, R., & Jamison, A. (1998). *Music and social movements: Mobilizing traditions in the twentieth century*. Cambridge, GB: Cambridge University Press.

Lieberman, R., & People's Songs (Organization). (1989). *My song is my weapon: People's Songs, American communism, and the politics of culture, 1930–1950*. Urbana: University of Illinois Press.

Lomax, A., Guthrie, W., & Seeger, P. (2012). *Hard hitting songs for hard-hit people*. Lincoln: University of Nebraska Press.

Marshall, L. (2007). *Bob Dylan: The never ending star*. Cambridge, GB: Polity.

Mitchell, G. (2007). *The North American folk music revival: nation and identity in the United States and Canada, 1945–1980*. Burlington, VT: Ashgate Publishing, Ltd.

Reuss, R., & Reuss, J. (2000). *American folk music and left wing politics.1927–1957*. Lanham, MD: The Scarecrow Press.

Seeger, P., & Blood, P. (1993). *Where have all the flowers gone: A singer's stories, songs, seeds, robberies*. Bethlehem, PA: Sing Out.

Weissman, D. (2005). *Which side are you on? An inside history of the folk music revival in America*. New York, NY: Continuum.

Chapter Three

Phish and the Spirit of Woodstock

A Woodstock Moment

When a fan posted on a Phish Facebook page that "we had a Woodstock moment at *SPAC* last week," everyone who read the post knew exactly what was meant. *SPAC* is the Saratoga Performing Arts Center, located about as close as you can get to the original Woodstock site, on Yasgur's 600 acre farm in the small, upstate New York farming community of Bethel—near the town of Woodstock. Phish has performed at SPAC every year since 1990 (except for 1993)—and often two or three nights in a row—making it the band's most well-known and revered venue, its "home field" if you will. For many Phish fans this is hallowed ground, and the best that can be expected from a Phish concert or festival is that it provide a few, brief "Woodstock moments," a few moments when everything comes together, flowing naturally and spontaneously, providing participants with a sense of community and identity that supports individual differences and freedom, and facilitates spiritual experiences. Significantly, the peak experience of Woodstock, and a Phish concert, is identified with moments, and thus with a dwelling *within* the moving moment, and a transcending of the normal, everyday understanding of time and reality. The "Woodstock moment" is, in these terms, another variation and further development of Kerouac's notion of "IT." As explained in Chapter One, "IT" was explored in *On the Road* and would become a central aspect of beat cultural politics. This suggests that the late Sixties Woodstock generation inherited much from its "parent" beat generation, and that this inheritance has been passed on to Phish fans.

The counterculture of the late Sixties was also indebted to the folk revival in important ways. Far more than the beat culture, the counterculture of the late 1960s carried on the idealistic project of the Sixties, tied now to a language of social transformation through a radical love and communalism; and this was to result primarily from a change in consciousness rather than a take-over of the state and its apparatuses of control. The revolution was not to be about gaining political power so much as changing the way people think, desublimating and redirecting their desires, and bringing them together in peace, love, and freedom. In this, the counterculture differed significantly from the radical activist movement, represented for example by Students for a Democratic Society (SDS), that had moved toward a confrontational politics vis-à-vis the "police state" and embraced a revolutionary ideology that was anti-capitalist, anti-colonial, anti-racist, and anti-sexist. The counterculture movement did come with a politics, but they were a politics of consciousness and everyday life, and of a *radical love* that was to save people and set them free. This locates the counterculture within a long history of cultural romanticism, with its utopianism, its emphasis on the power of the imagination, and its critique of the narrow technical rationality of the modern age. The counterculture in this sense (at least potentially) was a radical, even revolutionary movement, for it challenged the hegemony of capitalism, and of mass production commodity consumption.

E. F. Schumacher's "Small is Beautiful" expressed the counterculture's belief that people needed to return to more ecological, less consumer-driven, more self-sustaining communities, with people returning to craft production technologies and economies. All of this was designed to create a way of life in which people were free to develop their fuller potentials and overcome the chilling effects of alienation from each other and the natural world. It is important to remember that at the time of the Woodstock festival, many had come to believe that the counterculture would usher in a new age: often called the Age of Aquarius. Significantly, the Woodstock festival was billed as "an Aquarian Exposition," a festival of "peace, love, and music," and to many the festival was taken as a sign that the cultural revolution, a revolution of new consciousness and a new way of living together in peace and love, had begun, and that the age of Aquarius was at hand. That hopefulness would not last long, but it was alive and well in the summer of 1969, and a younger, counterculture generation was leading the way.

When Phish plays at SPAC, spatially locating itself near Yasgur's farm, and when fans speak of a "Woodstock moment," they are speaking of a culture that began to flower, if only briefly, at Woodstock, and that has never entirely disappeared, in spite of efforts to commercialize and incorporate it within the dominant or hegemonic order, and has been passed down from the Woodstock generation to several generations of Phish fans now. What has not, and cannot, be passed down from one generation to the next is the particular historical and cultural context of Woodstock. Joni Mitchell's *Songs to Aging Children Come*, released a few months before Woodstock, expresses well the feeling of many young people at the time. They had grown up in a tumultuous decade, under the threat of nuclear annihilation, in a racially divisive country of violent confrontations and burning cities in both the South and North, with the assassination of the symbols of idealism and hope (John and Robert Kennedy and Martin Luther King, Jr.) and with the personal threat of having to serve in an unjust war in Vietnam or evade the draft in some way. All of this prematurely aged the generation that grew up in the Sixties; and by the time they got to Woodstock, they were old beyond their years, determined to recapture their youth—their sense of play, innocence, the unleashing of the imagination and the desublimation of desire—and link all this to a radical democratic politics of social transformation. Woodstock briefly recaptured, at the end of the decade, the politics of hope with which the decade began. Rock music historian Don Aters has observed of the Woodstock generation, of which he is a part, that the migration to Woodstock was a gathering of "Rainbow Warriors." "We were communal, culturally diverse, and in search of universal peace through the music that defined our generation" (Littleproud & Hague, 2009, p. 10). In spite of the cultural wars raging in America, the war in Vietnam, and the power of the military-industrial complex, Aters writes that "it seemed to us that cultural acceptance was imminent, and that music would be the universal elixir" (Ibid.).

As in the beat and folk revival movements, music came to play a central and defining role in the counterculture movement of the late 1960s through mid-1970s, and it is not really possible to separate the music from counterculture beliefs and cultural politics. That music, by 1967, was being called "rock" to distinguish it from "rock n' roll," which had become highly commercialized and programmed for a top 40 market of singles, targeted primarily to a high school audience of romantic girls and boys who liked surfing and surfer girls (along with muscle cars). Of course, rock n' roll included the Motown Sound, but in spite of the genius of artists like Stevie Wonder and Marvin Gaye, most of what came out of Motown was hit driven and assembly line produced, with artists having little control over their music. Rock music, by contrast, was taken seriously by a new generation of music critics who wrote for *Rolling Stone*, *Crawdaddy*, and the *Village Voice*. They used "rock" to describe the new counterculture-oriented music by *avant garde* bands and artists, and sometimes referred to this music as "rock fusion," which implied a hybrid music created by fusing together a number of different genres, both old and new—the blues, country, folk, rock n' roll, jazz, Indian, and psychedelia. In this regard, the music of Woodstock and the counterculture was a rejection of the prime directive of the folk revival: to work within established and separate folk traditions and forms.

By contrast, the rock artists of the counterculture were *avant garde*, always experimenting with and blending forms to create something entirely new and unique. The Beatles were leaders in this regard, and in their development of concept albums that developed complex themes, beginning with *Sgt. Pepper's Lonely Hearts Club Band*. Miles Davis is another good example of a musician who deliberately sought to break out of established formats and musical genres, in this case through a fusion of jazz, rhythm and blues, and psychedelia. Richard Gehr, in *The Phish Book*, writes that Phish has come to resemble Miles Davis, "specifically the electric Miles ... that revolutionized jazz-rock fusion between 1968 and 1975. Miles had heard the [Grateful] Dead, and vice versa, and was for a time jazz's most fascinating interpreter of the psychedelic imperative" (Gehr, 1998, p. 88). The new concept albums found an audience on the newly developed network of FM radio stations, often commercial-free, that played albums in their entirety, or played extended tracks from albums.

More generically, Phish is often identified as a jam band, a term that came into popular use only in the Nineties, to refer to bands like the Grateful Dead and Phish that had a devoted fan base or community, organized around "live" concert and festival performances that provided a context for improvisational "jams." Jam bands, consequently, may be appreciated as organically linked to the rock fusion and jazz fusion movements of the late 1960s, and Phish has made this link overt by "covering" a number of artists and songs performed at Woodstock, including: Credence Clearwater Revival's *Proud Mary*, Sly and the Family Stone's *Stand!*, Jimi Hendrix's *Isabella* and *Fire*, and Bob Dylan's song *I Shall be Released*, performed separately by Joan Baez and Joe Cocker, The Who's *Sparks, My Generation*, and *We're Not Gonna Take it*. In 1992, Phish toured extensively with Santana, whose California-Latin rock improvisational style first caught the attention of the public at Woodstock. While Phish has never performed any of the five songs that The Grateful Dead played at Woodstock, Trey Anastasio performed that set in its entirety at Bethel Woods as a guest of Phil Lesh & Friends in 2006. All of this points to the incredible diversity represented by late Sixties rock, and Phish adds to this diversity each time it covers a song by giving it a unique Phish twist, a unique style and sound, in a unique, never-to-be-repeated concert setting.

Rock fusion's celebration of cultural difference and diversity was expressive of wider cultural shifts going on, particularly among the young, away from monoculturalism and toward multiculturalism and cultural hybridity. The counterculture generation had lived through the civil rights era at an impressionable age, and also lived through the struggles of other people of color, women, and by the summer of 1969, gay men and lesbians (the Stonewall riots were only a month before Woodstock). The normative culture in the 1950s through early 1960s had been thoroughly Eurocentric and "White," with "minorities" either invisible within the mass media and American history, or assimilated into the racial Other with their differences erased. The counterculture had pretty well worked through and critiqued the limitations of monoculturalism as an oppressive worldview and ideology.

These limitations and contradictions had to do with an imperative to erase differences by assimilating them into a normative culture in which people supposedly have risen above "seeing" race, gender, and so on, yet at the same time exaggerate differences through continued reliance on what the Black feminist Patricia Hill-Collins calls "controlling images" that keep marginalized identity groups in their places at the margins, and in a subordinated role vis-à-vis the dominant culture. Race, class, gender, and sexual identity "Others" were either treated as just like "normal," or "regular" (i.e., White, middle class, heteronormative) people, in which case difference is erased in a normalizing discourse, or they were represented as representatives of "Otherness," with their differences from "normal" folks exaggerated. The counterculture youth of the late Sixties, and the rock music of the times, sought a way out of this monocultural trap by allowing "Others" to speak and perform for themselves, outside of controlling images of what the dominant culture expects them to be, but also in a way that encouraged the further development of cultural hybridity. This was a pluralism in which different identity groups are not seen as having completely separate or autonomous cultural traditions. Instead, they are understood to have developed in relation to each other, in a dynamic rather than static cultural context, and within an overall unity.

As Todd Gitlin has observed of counterculture youth of the Sixties, "they honored the unity-in-diversity of the human project" (Gitlin, 1993, p. xxii). This put the counterculture in opposition to movements that were organized around what has since been called "identity politics," based on belief in an authentic, essential basis for an uncontaminated identity. From the perspective of identity politics, music is (for example) either Black or White music, and never the twain will or should meet. By contrast, the music of Woodstock is what might be called hybrid multiculturalism, in which a mix of musical traditions is recognized, but none is understood as adhering to rigid identity or genre categories. Jimi Hendrix provides a good example of the multicultural hybridity that characterized fusion rock. Some Black critics have argued that Hendrix was not "Black" because of his failure to work in a Black musical tradition, others that he was a Black musician who played the blues, and indeed he was brought up listening to blues music in Seattle's Black community and began his career by performing the blues and rhythm-and-blues for Black audiences in the South. For Hendrix (at least by the time he went to England and formed the Jimi Hendrix Experience), and for his largely White, counterculture fan base, his music transcended genres and race and almost defined psychedelic music. Hendrix always refused to allow normative conceptions of Blackness (within both White and Black communities) to define him and determine what kind of music he wrote and performed; and while he was defined as Black in a White culture (in which one drop of Black blood made you Black), he was in fact part Black, Cherokee, and White, and his hybrid identity served to unsettle rather than reify established categories of race (Cross, 2005, p. 98). Of course, the counterculture was primarily White and middle class, so there was more racial and cultural diversity on the stage at Woodstock than there was in the audience. Still, the shift away from a discourse of monoculturalism and toward a discourse of multiculturalism and cultural hybridity was both radical and necessary, and it marked the Woodstock generation as distinct from earlier generations.

Large rock concerts and festivals, such as Woodstock and the earlier Monterey Pop Festival held in June 1967, offered semi-autonomous "free spaces," or perhaps more accurately liminal spaces both inside and outside the dominant culture, spaces of partial and limited freedom, where young people could enact new, countercultural forms of family and community and practice new modes of associated living. Nadine Caouette has observed of the Monterey Music Festival that it "brought together many different genres to create the first Pop festival"—including everything from soul music to psychedelic music, from commercial pop to folk music, from political music to music designed to "expand consciousness" (Caouette, 2014, p. 190).

Certainly, the shift to live concert and festival performances of rock music was on one level a practical and pragmatic development related to the incentive to maximize profits by promoters. There was more money to be made in big venues, although it is significant in this regard that the Monterey Pop Festival was a free concert, and its promoters were committed to the idea of a non-commercial counterculture. Woodstock too became a free concert after the organizers could no longer control admission, and part of the allure of the Woodstock story is that the festival was not supposed to be primarily to make money but rather to advance a cause. Of course, much money has been made out of Woodstock and out of the selling of the myth, from the albums of Woodstock music, to the 1970 documentary movie, *Woodstock*, to the 2009 Hollywood movie, *Taking Woodstock*, although ironically, these movies reproduced the notion that it was not about the money.

Indeed, rock festivals were a response to less pecuniary interests. By 1967 the counterculture movement was growing quite quickly, and festival settings allowed space for an expanding counterculture community to gather. As Bruce Pollock has observed in his history of the Woodstock festival, "this new counterculture quickly grew beyond the walls of the college gymnasiums and renovated movie theaters accustomed to housing them, exploding into the open fields at 100,000 a pop at outdoor festivals through the summer [of 1969]" (Pollock, 2009, p. xiii). Once young people attended a rock festival, they also were more likely to identify with counterculture communities and families that came together at festivals.

According to rock historian Michael Kramer, "friendship increasingly replaced kinship and sometimes even substituted for it" as a basis for identity and affiliation (Kramer, 2013, p. 10). Kramer argued that rock festivals and concerts were "induction centers" for identification with the counterculture. He borrowed this metaphor from *Crawdaddy* music critic Paul Williams who, writing in 1967, referred to the Fillmore Theatre in San Francisco as an "induction center," a parody of the military's induction centers that were then processing young men for service in Vietnam. The Fillmore was, within this context, to be understood as a counterculture induction center. Williams wrote that "the teenyboppers, college students, the curious adults come down to the Fillmore to see what's going on, and they do see and pretty soon they're part of it" (Ibid., p. 3). They left with a new sense of community and possibility—a spirit that was spreading among America's youth.

One could say something similar about Phish concerts and festivals. Many if not most Phish fans had little idea of what to expect when they went to their first Phish concert with friends or an older sibling, but they soon were inducted into a new community—"Newbies" in Phish language. Finally, live concerts and festivals were important for the counterculture because a true "Woodstock moment," a peak experience, was only possible when the lights were flashing and the music blaring, with a sea of fans moving to the music, and with psychedelics fueling spiritual experiences and visions. Of course, critics of rock festivals and concerts have noted that they are places where many young people are inducted into drug-centered communities and families, and it is certainly true that drugs, and the selling of drugs, became part of the rock concert and festival scene; and that many fans have heeded the call of Jimi Hendrix to become "experienced." At the same time, rock fans, including Phish fans, distinguish between the use and abuse of drugs, and also going to a concert "straight" or drug-free, and they affirm the freedom of each individual to choose among these options in an environment that is non-judgmental. This supports the counterculture principle of maximizing individual freedom and difference, even the freedom to abuse drugs.

Making of a Counterculture

In late August 1969, just two weeks after Woodstock, Theodore Roszak's *The Making of a Counter Culture: Reflections on the Technocratic Society and Its Youthful Opposition* was published by a major trade publisher, Doubleday, and marketed to a mass audience in the U.S. Roszak is generally given credit for coining the term "counter culture" to describe the youthful oppositional movement aimed a transforming society through change in consciousness and in how people relate to one another in everyday life. *The Making of a Counter Culture* was one of the first efforts by a respected social critic on the democratic Left to take the movement in youth culture seriously, arguing for the democratic transformative potential of the movement while also acknowledging its limitations and contradictions. Roszak put forward a defense of the counterculture from a position of an insider-outsider. He was an academic who had grown up in the fertile environment of Southern California's human potential and humanistic psychology movements. And he linked these to a cultural politics that was pacifistic and ecological.

In 1964, a 31-year-old Roszak left his position as a history professor at Stanford to become editor of *Peace News* in London, where he supported pacifism as a universalistic principle and the anti-nuke movement as an activist response. He also became familiar with the early "hippie" movement in the U.K., which had its counterpart in the U.S. That is where things were really beginning to happen, so in 1965 he decided to leave his position as editor of *Peace News* to return to America to begin a long academic career at California State University at Hayward, during which he emerged as an important public intellectual for the counterculture, beginning with naming it as a "counter" (oppositional and alternative) culture, and consequently as revolutionary rather than merely reformist in its potential.

By the time of the 1967 "Summer of Love" celebration in San Francisco, Roszak recognized that the movement was growing rapidly, and that while the youth who gathered in San Francisco that summer primarily wanted to play, unleash their desires, and celebrate their freedom, they were guided, even in their play, by a vision of a good society that was radically democratic. In a 2007 Public Broadcast Service (PBS) documentary on the Summer of Love, Roszak observed that the world envisioned by youth that summer was "a world where people lived gently on the planet without the sense that they have to exploit nature or make war upon nature in order to find basic security." It would be based on a "simpler way of life" that is more rural and less urban, "less consumption-oriented," and with greater value placed on spirituality, companionship, friendship, community.

In the supportive environment of San Francisco, and as a witness to what was happening there, Roszak finished his critique of mainstream "technocratic society" and his counterculture manifesto for change, published as *The Making of a Counter Culture*, and since that book was published within a few weeks of the Woodstock festival, it provided an immediate democratic progressive framework for interpreting that festival and assessing its significance. By reviewing Roszak's framework, it is also possible to conclude something about the continuing relevance of the late Sixties counterculture and its values, particularly within the Phish community.

Roszak began by cautioning against thinking of the counterculture as anything like a unified movement with which most American youth identified. Instead, he meant to treat the counterculture as a minority movement among young people and relatively small group of adult mentors. It excluded the quite large block of conservative youth—the Young Republican fraternity and sorority types—along with the liberal youth still clinging to the "Kennedy style" of idealism. It also excluded "old-line" Marxist youth activists who, according to Roszak, "continue to tend the ashes of the proletarian revolution." More importantly, for Roszak, the counterculture excluded "militant black young, whose political project has become so narrowly defined in ethnic terms" (1995, p. xii). The counterculture that emerges is White and middle class, and its cultural politics are those of a particular block within the White middle class fed up with conformity and alienation, and with the rewards of being privileged (commodity consumption). Roszak misses entirely what I have already said is one of the most important legacies of the counterculture—a belief in multiculturalism and diversity, and in cultural hybridity. Even if the counterculture was a youth culture of primarily White, middle class, privileged youth, it did attract some youth of color and (later) working class youth and as I have said, its values provided some basis for bringing young people together across their differences without at the same time erasing those differences. Still, the fact that the Sixties counterculture was overwhelmingly White and middle class speaks to the difficulty in 1969 (and unfortunately still today) of living or practicing these beliefs in multiculturalism and hybridity within American youth culture.

The counterculture has been a college and suburban-based phenomenon, and this has meant that it is not a movement that has bridged the working class-middle class gap—except for the period of the Sixties when a college education was relatively inexpensive, even free in California and New York State. The result was a huge surge in the number of young people from working class or farming backgrounds who were enrolled in college, right alongside of the more traditional college students from professional-managerial backgrounds. Large segments of the upwardly mobile White working class were thus exposed to counterculture influences on college campuses. This radicalized the counterculture, for youth from working class or lower middle class backgrounds were far more likely than their more privileged peers to believe the "establishment" had to be challenged.

Roszak put forward a generational theory of social change and revolution, rather than a class theory, and indeed the notion of a generation with a special mission and destiny makes some sense, especially in reference to the Boomer generation that came of age in the Sixties. That generation was produced as such within a discourse as the great "generation gap", a great cultural divide that separated the post-World War II (WWII) generation of young people from their parents' culture and that transformed the young into bearers of needed change. According to Roszak, "alienated young are giving shape to something that looks like fthe saving vision our endangered civilization requires" (1995, p. 1). But without a base outside of youth culture (a popular counterculture slogan was "don't trust anyone over 30") the counterculture could not establish the basis for a broad-based democratic reconstruction of American society. But the counterculture needed to do more than become more inter-generational; it also needed to connect with working class people and develop a class politics. Roszak tends to be dismissive of the Marxist theory that guided many New Left activists, such as those within SDS, which he associates with dogmatism, orthodoxy, "an institutionalized left-wing legacy," (1995, p. 2) and outdated discourses of revolution that involve overthrowing the state. Certainly, Roszak represents an important critique of the limits of Marxist orthodoxy among New Left activists in the late Sixties. At the same time, without some critique of capitalism and class inequalities, the counterculture was left with the vague hope that middle class youth could be a revolutionary force on their own.

Without a theory of capitalism and class, the counterculture fell back upon a theory that Roszak called *technocratic society*. From this perspective, the establishment was made up of specialized experts, professionals schooled to think in terms of precise plans, rules and regulations, working within hierarchical authority structures in bureaucratic institutions. This is yet another variation on C. Wright Mills notion of a *managerial society*, and Max Weber's notion of *bureaucratic authority*. The assumption is that both government and big business are organized along the same lines of efficiency and the rationalization of authority through rules and procedures. Objective consciousness, as Roszak calls it, takes over, so that unless something can be studied, analyzed, and produced following scientific methods of objectivity and detachment, and reduced to quantifiable terms, it doesn't really exist. Within such a society, citizens have to defer "to those who know better" (the experts and managers) (1995, p. 7). So people experience a lack of agency. They also experience alienation in their working lives and their lives as consumers of commodities, cut off by objective consciousness from the magical, the spiritual, the ecstatic, and the poetic. It is this alienation that supposedly will lead the young to lead a revolution to restore a way of life in which people are attuned to nature, not ruled by the clock and rigid schedules, not "slaves to the traffic light" (the title of a Phish song), and able to engage in work that is artistic, expressive, and self-fulfilling. This is insightful, and the notion of alienation certainly connects this critique with Marxist theory. But in this case, middle class youth are positioned as most alienated and therefore most revolutionary, precisely because they want more out of life than the commodities, and the social status, their privilege can buy. This view of the middle class, rather than the traditional working class, as the revolutionary class was pervasive in the counterculture, and it has continued to be influential among some post-Marxists.[1] But it would prove unrealistic to sustain the hope that White, middle class college students—the kind Roszak was talking about—could become a revolutionary force for cultural transformation without developing alliances with workers and people of color, or becoming more inter-generational in their cultural politics. In fact, the counterculture hippies and protesting students, with their anti-authority politics, their flaunting of conventional morality and gender roles, and the economic privilege which they took for granted, never gained the support of large sectors of the working class in America, which turned toward cultural conservatism at least partially in reaction to the counterculture.

If the counterculture was influenced by Marx, according to Roszak, it was by the young Marx of the *Economic and Philosophical Manuscripts*, before Marx became an economic determinist and learned to speak and write in the language of objectivism. This early Marx emphasized a critique of human consciousness over the material base (the economy), and this included a theory of alienation and "species being" that was consistent with the counterculture. This is also the Marx that Roszak concludes most informs Herbert Marcuse, one of the great intellectuals of the counterculture movement of the late sixties. Marcuse wove together Marx and Freud—Gilles Deleuze and Felix Guattari were also doing this in France—to produce a radical psychoanalytic Marxism that shifted attention away from an analysis of the economic base to the realm of what Marx had called the *superstructure*, the realm of consciousness formation and ideas. Freud, in *Civilization and Its Discontents* and *Beyond the Pleasure Principle*, argued that civilization could only be built, and progress made in subduing nature, by the repression of the *pleasure principle* and its sublimation in the form of work or labor. Growing up was a form of becoming civilized. It required learning to be guided by the "reality principle," a scientific and technical rationality, and a normative institutional mindset that Marcuse called *one-dimensional*. Freud had argued that people submitted to the repressive sublimation required in modern civilization because that civilization offered them much in return. It they could only learn to defer and sublimate their desires, they could get back security and wealth, and pursue their desires more than if they lived in an insecure, uncivilized, barbaric state. Freud never recognized this as a very good bargain, but believed it was the best bargain we could make.

In *Eros and Civilization*, Marcuse accepted Freud's basic argument that the building of modern, industrial, "civilized" culture had required a good deal of repression of desire and its sublimation into work; but Marcuse argued that technology was now making possible Marx's dream, the replacement of routine, industrial work by robotic technology, so that humans could be free to explore their desires and participate in the creative production of self and culture. Since the 1950s and 1960s, these robotic machines have become ever more sophisticated and prevalent in the industrial production of commodities, and in a different way in the service industry economy. This begs two questions: *Why are people experiencing an intensification of their working lives?* and, *Why have most people not reaped the rewards of leisure and creative self-development?* Marcuse's answer is that in advanced capitalism, discipline and authority over workers is maintained through *surplus repression*, that additional repression beyond what is actually needed in the economy, the family, and other institutions, but which is needed in order to maintain relations of domination and privilege. We might think of the late 1960s in the U.S. as characterized by the growth of a leisure culture and increases in leisure time particularly within the middle classes, and simultaneously the continuation of a culture of surplus repression and disciplinary power. In these terms, the youthful counterculture was a reaction formed against surplus repression, and also an assertion of leisure pursuits and desires as important in identity formation.

Rock music and the counterculture not only was an expression of the new culture of leisure in the U.S. among the middle class, it was also a rejection of surplus repression. Rather than submit to the authority relations of the workplace, and to the discipline of routinized and regimented work processes, counterculture youth sought to opt out of the mainstream economy and become craft workers, selling their wares in counterculture economies and living more simply and basically, demystifying the power of money and wealth. The Phish community supports such an alternative craft economy of Phish wares, at concerts and festivals and also online; and this economy is part of a Phish philosophy, a way of living authentically and unplugging yourself from mainstream economy.

Of course, the counterculture was only one counter-formation among American youth. The other was a youth culture oriented toward using leisure time, and satisfying libidinal desires, through the consumption of mass-produced commodities. In this case, leisure time and pursuits are compensatory, providing relief from a working world experienced as drudgery, alienating, oppressive. Marcuse recognized that advanced capitalism had learned to exploit the leisure time market by encouraging what he called *repressive desublimation*. This involves allowing, even encouraging, people to unrepress their desires, and then channeling those desublimated desires toward commodity consumption. The example Roszak offers is of the Playboy philosophy and publishing empire, selling commodified images of objectified sexuality, in which sexual partners are objects to be used and discarded, in which real human intimacy gets reduced to sexual voyeurism and fantasy. Roszak writes that in a Playboy culture, "the woman becomes a mere playmate, a submissive bunny, a mindless decoration ... half the population is reduced to being the inconsequential entertainment of technocracy's pampered elite" (1995, p. 15). Repressive desublimation in sexual terms is represented by the whole commodification of desire that is on exhibit in shopping malls and in the mass media, so that people's desires are met by shopping, or at least they are briefly satiated. A female college student once told me that whenever she was depressed or over stressed by her course assignments, she went shopping and bought something, and that almost immediately she felt better.

But repressive desublimation cannot entirely compensate for, and in fact furthers, the alienation of the individual since it plugs the individual into a commodity consumption economy, which is itself alienating and does not meet people's authentic needs. According to Roszak this means that those must be integrated into technocratic society, climbing up the competitive organizational hierarchy, and in their leisure time playing with their high-priced "toys"—fancy clothes, cars, houses, yachts—are the most alienated, and thus ultimately the most potentially radical. He writes for example that "alienation, properly understood, has been more heavily concentrated in the upper levels of capitalist society than in its long-suffering depths" (Roszak, 1995, p. 96). This assertion, beyond what Marcuse would have said, flies in the face of reason and history and leads Roszak to make some astonishing statements. The revolution to free us from alienation is thus not to be led by the working class or poor but by privileged young people who experience alienation in their own lives and witness it in their parents' lives, and who want something better. If this belief in the revolutionary potential of middle class youth is naive, it did spur a generation of primarily middle class youth to believe they were a revolutionary force, and to imagine they could bring on a new, Aquarian age that would free everyone from alienation. And because they thought of themselves as a revolutionary generation—although they were a distinct minority of American youth—they did become a revolutionary class of sorts, establishing a fundamental shift in culture, and an alternative or counter space for speaking and acting that was in some ways transformative. If this reads as a qualified assessment of the counterculture it is because revolutionary movements are associated with the oppressed and the subaltern. But the argument that the revolutionary class is not the traditional industrial working class but rather a new middle class of information workers, has become more influential since both Marcuse's and Roszak's time.

Roszak reads Marcuse as undermining the later more class deterministic and scientific Marx by arguing that alienation originated out of a pre-historical, primordial fall from grace. Indeed, for the early Marx, humans' original and authentic state is living as part of the natural world, and relating to each other as fellow humans, as part of a collective community. Whatever might be said about the historical validity of these claims, Marx used this originary state of grace, this Garden of Eden-like starting point for the development of human culture. He argued that if we work hard, submit to authority, and further develop the forces of capitalist production, we will slowly evolve to the point where a counter-capitalist or socialist alternative emerges, followed by the realization of a utopian communism that would usher in the "end of history."

In most ways, Marcuse and Roszak are in agreement. But Roszak breaks with Marcuse on the necessity of waiting for the end of history to realize utopia. For Marx, and for Marcuse, true liberation must emerge out of the further rationalization of the "anarchy of production," out of the heightened development of the social and technical relations of production under capitalism. From this perspective, communist utopia would only emerge from out of the furthest possible development of industrial, capitalist, forces of production, and only after nature had been further "subdued" and made to serve utilitarian aims. Only then would its dialectical Others, socialism and communism, be realized. The trouble with this, as Roszak and other postmodern theorists have argued following Nietzsche rather than Marx, is that people are asked to put up with alienation—to give up freedom—with the hope that someday in the distant future a society would be built in which people would live free and non-alienating lives. This was not a bargain worth making, according to Nietzsche—or Dostoevsky. *Notes from the Underground* (1983), Dostoevsky's most philosophical novel, became an essential text in the counterculture canon. He writes of a man who symbolically has gone underground and developed a critique of both the bourgeois dominant culture and the Marxist and pre-Marxist revolutionaries who were emerging in Russia at that time. Dostoevsky writes that both of these ideologies offered variations on a common mythology of progress. According to this mythology, if people worked hard and submitted to authority and discipline, someday they would inherit a "crystal palace." Of course, in the meantime they had to keep living for a bit longer in "chicken coops" with leaking roofs. Dostoevsky's Underground Man began to think it was all a lie, that the Chrystal Palace would not be coming, and the chicken coops would keep getting drabber. For Roszak, to "postpone until 'later' consideration of the humanly essential in the name of 'being realistic' is to practice the kind of deadly practicality which now stand our civilization in peril of annihilation" (Roszak, 1995, p. 101). The counterculture would not wait for its utopia, and utopia would not come in the form of a Crystal Palace built by technocracy.

Instead, Roszak suggests that cultural transformation would take the form of a re-spiritualization and a re-enchantment of the world, and a return to magical consciousness—along with a desublimation of desires. That is, the Aquarian age is to represent a return to the past, in this case, an originary past, that is, an imaginary past of original consciousness before magical ways of knowing were banished from modern culture by objective consciousness. The revival of the pleasure principal, consequently, was to be about much more than the unleashing of libidinal desires alone, although the sexual revolution was to be part it. For Roszak and others who identified with the counterculture, desire was also desire for reconnection to the natural, for transcendent spiritual experiences of connection to the universe and to nature, for communion with others, and for freedom of individuals to script their lives outside the institutions that seek to discipline and control them.

Significantly, Dionysian Productions, the name of Phish's production company, is an obvious reference to Nietzsche famous distinction between the Apollonian and the Dionysian. An early member of the Phish family, Ben Hunter, is credited with coming up with the name Dionysian Productions, and in an interview he observed: "Dionysian seemed to fit because we would often talk about our fondness for 'Dionysian reveling' ... I can't imagine the company being called anything but Dionysian Productions. It makes perfect sense given the sensibility of the company's one and only client" (Hunter, 2000, p. 674). The sensibility includes a preference for the "live" concert and festival experience, preferably under the stars in a natural setting, where, like the revelers in ancient Greek Dionysian festivals, Phish fans can get the whole package—have transcendent spiritual experiences, feel embraced in the oneness of community, and reconnect with what Nietzsche called the "will to power" (1968) and what Foucault called "practices of freedom" (1997, pp. 281–301).

Nietzsche, the Philosophy of Freedom

Conservative critics like Allan Bloom, who taught the "Great Books" as a humanities professor at the University of Chicago, felt that the "problem" of the late Sixties is that through permissive upbringing and rock n' roll, young college students had become too Dionysian, and surely this was a sign that the nation, the civilization, was in decline. Bloom's *The Closing of the American Mind*, published in 1987 during an era of a conservative restorational politics in American education when Phish was just beginning to organize its own counterculture community, was a national bestseller and it stirred a great debate between cultural conservatives like Bloom and progressives who defended a more student-centered and relevant curriculum. The philosophical villain in Bloom's narrative turns out to be Nietzsche rather than Marx, as one might expect. Bloom faults Nietzsche on two counts. First, Bloom accuses Nietzsche of promoting a form of relativism in which people feel free to create their own truths and values, and believe anything they want to believe, regardless of what their professors and the great thinkers of Western culture have had to say. It is accurate to say, I think, that the counterculture of the late 1960s, armed either implicitly or explicitly with this Nietzschean perspective, was not interested in learning about absolute transcendent truths and values passed down from centuries of philosophical, political, and religious discourse and encoded in canonical texts and authoritative lectures. They believed in the revaluing of all values, to use Nietzsche's language, and they demanded that everything they taught be made relevant to the revolution, and what's happening today at the university. That attitude can be dismissive of the past, but it, against what Bloom said, is also a sign that the young understand that history is only a story, or stories, told about the past, from certain perspectives and set of interests, and that the trick is to construct what Foucault (1970) called a "history of the present," that begins with the present and the concerns of the present. Second, Nietzsche had argued that music could release the Dionysian impulse in people, which had a subversive, liberatory, democratic power. But for Bloom, both rock and jazz create a kind of delirium of the soul, an unleashing of desire, and ultimately mind control that makes a liberal college education almost impossible.

In an oft-quoted passage, Bloom argues that a history of great ideas and progress toward the rule of reason rather than passion, is reduced through rock music, to "a pubescent child whose body throbs with orgasmic rhythms; whose feelings are made articulate in hymns to the joys of onanism or the killing of parents, whose ambition is to win fame and wealth in imitating the drag-queen who makes the music" (Dettmar, 2006, p. 84; Freedman, 2000, p. 211). This is a rather amazing statement, but it does repeat the basic Platonic argument against music that cultural conservatives deployed; and we must return to the ancient Greeks to trace a genealogy of rock music back to the Dionysian spirit and Dionysian festivals, and to a liberatory and democratic cultural politics that helped serve as a balance against the authority, discipline, rules, reason, and duty associated with the god Apollo.

Nietzsche's thoughts on the Dionysian and the Apollonian spirits in ancient Greek culture are developed in his first book published in 1872, *The Birth of Tragedy from the Spirit of Music*. In that book, he put forward a dialectical argument where Greek culture developed out of the Apollonian and the Dionysian spirits, each constructed in opposition to the other. Later, Nietzsche would reject the idea of a dialectic leading to a progressive development of culture and replace it with a belief in the Greek ideal of balance, with both impulses understood to be necessary and not in conflict so long as they were kept in balance. The trouble, from this perspective, is that Western culture since Plato has placed a much greater emphasis on Apollo than on Dionysus and that the balance needs to be restored. To do this Nietzsche believed the Dionysian needed to be reasserted, and that this would restore vitality and creativity to Western culture. For without the Dionysian, Western culture had become a culture of alienation, despair and disconnection from the natural world. The crisis of Western culture in the late nineteenth century, as Nietzsche saw it, had to do with the repression of the Dionysian.

In *The Birth of Tragedy*, Nietzsche argued that Greek tragedy was, in the end, about teaching Apollonian virtues of submission to one's fate as the will of the gods. The heroes of Greek tragedy learn they are not in control of their own fate, that social order must be restored in the face of those who revolt against, or defy it. Even if tragic heroes are sympathetic, for they strive to be free, the social order and traditional values and moral codes are restored at the end of the play. Within the Greek tragedy, a chorus of muses (and the word "music" is derived from "muse") at the back of the stage helped narrate the play and also provide music that reflected the feelings being expressed by the actors. This, Nietzsche says, was Apollonian music. It adhered to rules, was highly scripted, disciplined, and controlled, and it was subordinated to the Apollonian play. Nietzsche recognized much of the classical European canon of music as Apollonian, an "architecture of sound," with Opera a prime example. But another tradition of music in ancient Greek culture pre-dated the birth of tragedy. That was a tradition of music associated with Dionysus, the god of wine, play, dance, and music, and it found expression in Dionysian festivals, often held in the spring to celebrate the rebirth of life and of the human spirit. Nietzsche wrote that "Dionysian stirrings arise either through the influence of ... narcotic potions ... or through the powerful approach of spring, which penetrates with joy the whole frame of nature" (1995, p. 3). In mass Dionysian festivals that often went on day and night for several days, the wine flowed and musicians wandered through the crowds playing their flutes and lyres and encouraging people to dance. In such a festival context, "not only does the bond between people come to be forged once more by the magic of the Dionysian rite, but nature itself, long alienated or subjugated, rises again to celebrate the reconciliation." Slaves are made free and all the inequalities that "either necessity or despotism has erected between people are shattered." People feel "at one" with their fellows, ecstatic in their "vision of mystical Oneness ... as the member of a higher community." People become "works of art," and the "productive power" of the universe surges through them (1995, pp. 22–24). So transformed, people break into a spontaneous, improvisational dance, in which they both express themselves individually and become part of a moving Oneness. Dance is for Nietzsche both a literal and a symbolic signifier of a creative, passionate, engagement with life, and whoever wants to be free must learn to dance. In *Thus Spake Zarathustra*, Nietzsche wrote that "a day in which you have not danced is a day you have wasted." *Zorba the Greek*, Nikos Kazantzaki's 1946 novel made into a movie in 1964, represents this Nietzschean wisdom. It is the story of a young, intellectual, rational, and ordered young man—an Apollonian spirit—who returns to Greece to take over a family business and slowly learns to live life as a dance, taught by Zorba, who represents the Dionysian spirit. The young man finally asks Zorba: "Teach me to dance." It is possible to witness this Dionysian dancing at any Phish concert, for as I have said, the "audience" becomes an active participant in the performance, moving to a music that pulses through them and lifts them up in an ecstatic Dionysian dance of life. I sometimes like to imagine what Nietzsche would say or do if he could be transported with a time machine to a Phish concert, and I suspect he would be dancing too; and he would see the collective revelry as a good sign, that the Dionysian spirit was still alive and well in the early 21st century.

Nietzsche was the philosopher of freeing yourself from the normative Apollonian order, which he thought of as a herd culture, where people were totally dominated and made submissive, herded around like cattle or sheep, lived according to a set of rules and routines (but at least were fed and cared for to keep them satisfied). In such a context, he believed, a revival of the Dionysian spirit was revolutionary, although Nietzsche did not see it on the horizon in the West. He often thought of himself as writing for a reader a century after he wrote, who might be more receptive to what he had to say. And it is prophetic that the very Dionysian Woodstock music festival would be held almost a century after *The Birth of Tragedy from the Spirit of Music*. In *Ecce Homo*, Nietzsche held out hope for a "Dionysian future of music." Encouraging the reader to "look ahead a century" when "two millennia of antinature and desecration of man" would be challenged by a Dionysian generation. "That new party of life which would tackle the greatest of all tasks, the attempt to raise humanity higher ... [and] make possible that excess of life on earth from which the Dionysian state, too, would have to awaken" (Nietzche, 1969, p. 271; Johnston, 2007, p. 52). The more Apollonian our culture became, the more it called into being a Dionysian counterculture to reestablish a needed balance.

In the summer of 1969, a mere month before Woodstock, the Apollo moon landing was accomplished as a supreme tribute to the power of Apollonian rationality, institutional authority, discipline, and objective consciousness. It was the crowning achievement of an Apollonian society, yet it ended up stirring the imagination of people around the globe, unleashing the Dionysian imagination. It is fitting then that Woodstock would follow the moon landing by a month, for both were often positioned as contiguous in time and manifestation of the same thing, the dawning of a new age of Aquarius. This was a dawning already envisioned mythologically in Stanley Kubrick's epic film, *2001: A Space Odyssey* (1968). The film uses psychedelic, light show images to represent a transformation of consciousness, human to transcend Apollonian excesses, represented in the film by HAL, the emotionally cool and rational, computer that finally has to be "unplugged" in order for Dave to evolve to a higher consciousness and state of being.

Pranksterism

One of the most iconic figures in the counterculture was Ken Kesey, celebrated author of two major novels, *Once Flew Over the Cuckoo's Nest* (1962) and *Sometimes a Great Notion* (1964). Both books speak to Kesey's counterculture philosophy, although they were written in quick succession years (that seemed like a decade) before Woodstock and the publication of Rosak's *Making of a Counterculture*, and over two decades from 1997, the year Kesey and his Merry Pranksters, traveling in the hippie bus "Further" (alternately spelled "Furthur"), finally met up with Phish, at Darien Lake, in upstate New York. Kesey had come a long way since the early 1960s, but he continued to embody the spirit of the counterculture in the decades ahead until he died in 2001. That spirit was there in his two major novels—the defiance of institutional power by rebellious, even revolutionary, figures like McMurphy in *One Flew Over the Cuckoo's Nest*, who clearly is another, updated version of the character Dean Moriarty. Significantly, Kesey would convince the "real life" Moriarty, Neil Cassady, to be the driver of Further on Kesey and his Pranksters, first tour of the country in the summer of 1964, from San Francisco to New York City to visit the World's Fair and to promote his second novel along the way. The bus, minus Kesey and Cassady, would also travel to Woodstock in the summer of 1969, where the Pranksters (particularly "Wavy Gravy") played a significant role in building a collective community spirit of helping one another.

In the summer of 1997, a "new" 1947 school bus called Furthur, which replaced the original bus, was ready for its first cross-country trip with Kesey and the Pranksters on board. They were off to induct Furthur into the Rock and Roll Hall of Fame in Cleveland, Ohio as a sixties artifact, and from Cleveland the bus full of Pranksters took off to pay a visit, and to prank Phish in one of its concerts. This would turn out to be the last cross-country trip for Further. Kesey's health was failing and he must have known his time was limited, so that visiting Phish and participating in one of their concerts might well have been for Kesey a way of coming home, the closest he could get to the feeling, the mood, and the consciousness of the late Sixties counterculture.

In 1964, Kesey was a well-known and respected author with an expected brilliant writing career ahead. But something happened along the way to change all that, and there is good reason to believe that something was psychedelic drugs, especially LSD, which as he later acknowledged had made him much more about living in the moment and experiencing life to the fullest. The character he assumed on the stage with Phish at Darien Lake—the Wizard of Oz, the prankster supreme—was the culmination of the persona he had created for himself, and lived, after he decided to follow the path of the prankster as a counterculture rebel.

The prankster is a troublemaker who disrupts the normal in ways that are unsettling, and that encourage people to question their everyday way of understanding the world. For example, the feminist philosopher and social theorist Judith Butler has argued that "drag," in which men dress as women in often comically exaggerated and stereotypical terms, is potentially subversive of gender norms because it is based in the audience understanding that gender is a performance, that it exists in a certain stylized presentation of the body, so that, Butler concludes, "the inner truth of gender is a fabrication and ... true gender is a fantasy instituted and inscribed on the surface of bodies" (Butler, 1990, p. 174). In a similar way, Kesey and the Merry Pranksters can be said to have parodied American fictional and "real life" characters in order to reveal the "real" for what it is, a fabrication and a fantasy, and that there is no objective social reality aside from the realities that people construct and perform. At Darien Lake, Kesey and the Pranksters dressed up as characters from *The Wizard of Oz*, but in their version the story was different from the original, and the movie, and spoofed the conventional or "normal" interpretation of the story as a morality tale, in which a young girl who has wandered off to a Technicolor fantasy land learns that "there's no place like home," the little Kansas town where she grew up, where everything (as Paul Simon would say) is black and white. In the Prankster version, the Wizard of Oz (Kesey) is a benign leader and chief prankster, a counterculture guru who calls on all pranksters to find each other, come together and embrace one another, and fight the forces of darkness that seek the subjugation of the human spirit.

The Pranksters had first come together in Marin County and San Francisco in the early 1960s, under the leadership of Kesey, and in the company of Jerry Garcia and The Grateful Dead. Together, they all played a powerful role in bringing a counterculture together in San Francisco, and in linking that counterculture to the embryonic experimental, acid rock music movement in the city. But in the beginning there was the first Further bus trip in 1964, a trip made famous by Tom Wolfe, the journalist of Now, in *The Electric Kool-Aid Acid Test*. Wolfe was both infatuated by Kesey as an Alpha Male and charismatic leader of a new movement among the young, and also critical of Kesey's self-indulgence and the "preposterous" widespread use of drugs, including "acid" or LSD, on the bus trip. But what stands out in the book, as Mark Christensen, Kesey's biographer, remarks is that "Wolfe describes a national accident about to happen, a clash of cultures old and new" (2010, p. 101). By "old," Wolfe meant the dominant, conventional culture, the culture of the technocracy and objective consciousness as Roszak put it. But for Kesey, the old and the new also referred to the old counterculture—the beats—and the new counterculture of hippies and psychedelia.

Neil Cassady was the corporeal link between the beats and the Sixties counterculture, and in asking him to drive the Merry Pranksters' bus "Further" on a cross-country trip, Kesey obviously meant to make a point. The Pranksters were the inheritors of the beats, but took beat culture further—hence the bus name. Kesey also thought of Cassady in a way that was no doubt inseparable from the character Dean Moriarty in Kerouac's *On the Road*. Kesey was Neil/Dean's psychological double: a charismatic, athletic, full of life, determined to live life outside the norms of the dominant culture, and committed to a form of transcendent "IT" experience as personally and socially transformative. When people began to experience living in the moment, as a moving stream or road, and to experience this moment as transcendent and magic, they would supposedly turn their backs on the time discipline of the clock and the corporate workplace, on the technical-rationality and mind-forged manacles of the "establishment" and demand to live authentically as creative, free spirits, on the road to "IT." This at least was the hope of Kesey and other utopians identified with the counterculture, even if Kerouac and the beats had not been so optimistic about transforming American culture, only finding a free space at the margins. Kesey had been introduced to Cassady when the latter began hanging out at Kesey's hangout near Stanford after getting out of San Quentin on a minor drug charge, and the two quickly became friends in a very different way than Cassady and Kerouac had become. Kerouac had been the writer outsider, the intellect, the man of reflection to Cassady's manic craziness, his lust for life and living in the moment. In contrast, Kesey and Cassady saw in each other similar types, even if Kesey also could play the reflective intellectual at times while Cassady was all action, moment, improvisational talk.

LSD or *acid* was the agent of social transformation for Kesey and the Pranksters, and for the emerging San Francisco counterculture scene in 1964. Psychedelic drugs had been unavailable to the beats in the 1950s, but they were becoming available by the early 1960s and were still not illegal, so the 1964 road trip by the Pranksters was designed to introduce America to the transformative power of LSD. Kesey had been introduced to LSD in the late 1950s as a participant in a CIA sponsored Army study on the uses of LSD in the interrogation of POWs and captured spies. Kesey enjoyed the irony that the CIA started the psychedelic counterculture when they introduced youth to LSD. In a 1981 interview[2] (along with Jerry Garcia) on The Tom Snyder program on NBC, Kesey explained: "I had a neighbor who was a psychologist and he was booked to do them [the LSD experiments] on Tuesday, and he chickened-out and asked me 'do you want to do them?' Show up, $20, I showed up, they gave 'em to me, and I did 'em for six or eight months. There were about 120 of us down in Palo Alto, students and un-students. The government wanted somebody to look in that room, they said, 'hey, we've got a great room ... just go in and look it over ... just don't let anyone else in that room.'" All of this was said with great Prankster humor and much laughter, as was Kesey's style. Later in the interview Snyder asks Kesey if he thinks he might have been hurt by his use of LSD, and Kesey responds with a goofy face, "Nah nah, nah nah, nah nah ..." and Garcia interjects, "so far," while Kesey goes on, "it's all right so far."

Again, all of this is said amid much collective laughter, spurred on by the head Prankster himself, who then, quite suddenly turns serious and becomes the intellectual who wrote two landmark novels. "Just for the sake of the record," he says, "I think you don't get anything for free. Everything bruises something. So you trade off." Garcia provides an example when Snyder asks him if we was able to function when he was playing on LSD. He says, "Well, not in the conventional way ... It's not something I would want to do professionally. Now I have more of a sense of responsibility to at least be able to be in command, to be able to play ... At lot of times [in the early 'Acid Test' Kesey and the Dead put on in San Francisco in the mid 1960s] we'd be really too high to play. We'd play for maybe a minute and then we'd lose it ... But when we did play we played with a certain kind of freedom you rarely get as a musician." That was because the audience came for the Acid Test more than the music, so the Dead didn't have to live up to any musical expectations in that regard, "So in terms of being able to experiment freely, it was amazing." Kesey, again as the serious intellectual, suggests that what was going on in the Sixties wasn't all about drugs. "There was a lot of other stuff going on at the same time, like the consciousness expansion area musically, artistically, and in drama ... I think it was the beginning of a real, true revolution that's still going on."

All of these features of the counterculture, from psychedelic drugs to the expansion of consciousness, were there from the beginning, when the Merry Pranksters went on the road in a 1939 International Harvester school bus named Further in the summer of 1964. This was also Freedom Summer, when young Black and White college students came together in Oxford, Ohio, to prepare themselves for a bus ride South, to help register Black voters—where three of the college students, two White and one Black would be murdered by the Ku Klux Klan. It was as if the Pranksters and the counterculture were from a different world than the politically motivated, folk music-oriented college students, with different cultural politics, and so Further would not stop on its cross-country trip for the Pranksters to lend support for civil rights protests and activities like Freedom Summer. As I already noted, the leaders of an emerging counterculture had more in common with the Beats than with the folk revival and the student protest movement that in 1964 was all about realizing the idealist dream of a racially just and equal society. Further and the Pranksters came out of San Francisco, and young people and their older leaders there were thinking about, and making, a cultural revolution in a very different way than the Freedom Summer participants, and the folk music protesters, were.

When Furthur and the Pranksters arrived in New York City, aside from a visit to the World's Fair, Kesey made it clear to his literary agent there that he wanted to meet Kerouac, who was at that time living with his mother on Long Island. A meeting was arranged and Cassady, along with Allen Ginsberg, Peter Orlovsky (Ginsberg's partner), and Peter's brother Julius, drove to Northport Long Island to get Kerouac and bring him to Manhattan. Sterling Lord, who was Kerouac's literary agent and became Kesey's agent as well, remembers: "Jack was 12 years older than Ken, and there was a marked difference in their energies and interests." Although he still had to deal from time to time with the public adulation inspired by the 1957 publication of *On the Road* he was leading "a relatively passive life." On the other hand, Lord writes that "Kesey and the Pranksters ... were on an extended high that peaked in New York. According to one of the Pranksters, Ken Babbs, every place they had stopped on the bus trip, they had gotten out their musical instruments, donned their regalia, turned on the cameras and tape recorders, and broken into 'spontaneous combustion musical and verbal make-believe shenanigans.'"[3] This was the context of the meeting between Kesey, a few other Prankers, and Kerouac in Kesey's Manhattan apartment. According to Lord, "There was absolutely no serious or colorful discussion between Kesey and Kerouac. Jack was never loud, or critical, or indignant. He seemed tired, but he was patient with the Pranksters' antics." Within an hour, Kerouac excused himself and exited, a bit overwhelmed and dismayed by what he had witnessed. Lord realized that Kerouac "was deeply committed to writing. Kesey was just as deeply committed to living and experiencing the lives of others; writing for him was just a part of living." But these were differences, for the most part, of personality rather than philosophy; and it is important to remember that in his day, Kerouac had gone on the road himself and learned to live life as well as to reflect on it.

The counterculture generation was the child of the Beat generation, and it inherited much from its "parents," much more than from the folk revival movement. But the counterculture would ultimately be recognized as a new, unique movement rather than a beat revival, and perhaps for that reason, Roszak, in seeking to define and characterize the counterculture, left out Kerouac and the beats entirely.

When Kesey and the Pranksters returned from New York City to San Francisco, they systematically set about the task of actually making a counterculture by creating venues for young people to gather and develop a distinctive and collective counter identity, and by editing a documentary film of the trip, pieced together from 30 hours of 16mm film that had been shot onboard Furthur. Wolfe described the "The Movie," as it was called, as "the world's first acid film, taken under conditions of total spontaneity barreling through the heartlands of America" (2008, p. 122). Unfortunately, the film would prove almost uneditable, because it included so much random and incoherent footage, including Cassady's nonstop improvisational babble, and also because the sound track was not synchronized with the film. Still, Kesey threw himself into the editing with an almost manic passion because he had decided that film would be his next medium, rather than writing. He said, "I am not a writer. I haven't written anything since I wrote those last drafts of [Sometimes a Great] Notion and I don't intend to write anything else ... To continue writing would mean that I couldn't continue my work [on the film]" (Mills, 2006, p. 94). Kesey's turn to film was ground-breaking in its own way. Kesey realized that films could reach a much wider audience than novels, and that film was more visceral in its impact. But he continued to struggle to create some order out of the chaos, to find a narrative in a series of seemingly unconnected moments, and that was a direct result of his use of "acid."

At the same time as he was editing "The Movie," Kesey began to stage fairly regular "acid tests" around San Francisco, initially at the homes of friends with invited guests, then later in large halls (like the Longshoreman's Hall on Beach Street) that Kesey rented. Whatever the venue, there was always lots of LSD-spiked punch available. As a prank, and to see how people would react when they thought they were high but really weren't, Kesey and the Pranksters occasionally left the LSD out of the punch, but that appeared to happen very rarely. After all, Kesey had become convinced that people needed to take acid in order to make the needed revolution in human consciousness. The acid tests also broke new ground in terms of creating an environment that was designed to encourage higher states of consciousness. Light shows were added, with flowing, psychedelic images projected on the walls, and strobe lights flashed colorful lights across the crowd. Finally, rock music was added. Jerry Garcia and his band the Warlocks, who would shortly become the Grateful Dead, served up psychedelic music to the crowd, and people moved in a spontaneous, improvisational dance. Dominick Cavallo writes that: "The acid tests were soirees of spontaneity. People confronted each other, displaying normally inhibited qualities of their personalities liberated by the drug." The purpose was to expose the "natural" self normally repressed, "to reveal the 'authentic' self that lay beyond the claims of convention, conformity and personality" (Cavallo, 2001, p. 112). Bill Graham entered the picture as producer of the acid tests, agreeing to work without reimbursement. He would bring together the technologies of the acid tests—the strobe lights and light shows, the computerized music, the experimental psychedelic rock music, and the hallucinogenic drugs to create something new, designed to provide a powerful, participatory experience for thousands of people. It was clear by 1965 that the counterculture was growing rapidly, and that its center was San Francisco. Over the next few years, Kesey would continue to be a leader in making things happen in San Francisco, from the Trips Festival in January, 1966 at the Longshoreman's Hall, "The Gathering of the Tribes" in Golden Gate Park in January 1967, up through the "Summer of Love" that year (Caouette, 2014, pp. 183–194). Along the way, he would flee to Mexico to avoid being prosecuted for possession of marijuana, return to San Francisco and be captured by the FBI, serve a few months in jail, and finally, in November 1967 return to Oregon. In February 1968, Kesey learned of Cassady's death in Mexico, which meant that Further would be left without a driver for its next cross-country trip (Dodgson, 2013, p. xxv).

Kesey and the Pranksters took Further on a pre-Woodstock road trip in June 1969, to participate in a solstice celebration held in New

Mexico on the reservation of the Tesuque Pueblo tribe. Shortly thereafter, Kesey and his family would leave for a trip to London, choosing to bypass the Woodstock Festival, perhaps because from Kesey's perspective, the East Coast was a least two years behind the West Coast in countercultural thinking, and so he did not expect anything new to happen at Woodstock that pushed the counterculture further. Instead, he chose to accept an offer from Zapple Records, an Apple Records subsidiary owned by the Beatles and intended for the release of spoken word, *avant garde* record albums. The Beatles had been much influenced by Kesey's 1964 road trip with Further, and their album and film, *Magical Mystery Tour* were attempts to mirror some of the magic of that 1964 trip. Once he arrived in London, Kesey was given a tape recorder and asked to wander around the city, recording his impressions for a spoken word album—a project that never went anywhere. As with "The Movie" of the 1964 bus trip, Kesey found that it was difficult to pull together a coherent narrative out of the chaos that confronted him in London, and he soon returned home to Springfield, Oregon, where he would withdraw from the world he had created for a few years, focusing on his family, and even going so far as to kick the Pranksters off his property when they returned from Woodstock.

Consequently, the Pranksters had to make the trip to Woodstock on their own, and given that Kesey's personality was so dominant, it allowed the Pranksters to speak for themselves and organize their own participation in the festival. Ken Babbs, a longtime Prankster, arranged for approximately 60 Pranksters and hangers-on to attend the festival, even if there wasn't room on the bus for them all (Miller, 1999, 20). Wavy Gravy, aka Hugh Romney, played a significant role once they got to the festival. When the Woodstock organizers asked him to handle food preparation and crowd security for Woodstock, he responded by rounding up 85 hippies from the Hog Farm commune, along with 15 Hopi Indians, and bringing them to New York (Reynolds, 2009, p. 224). At Woodstock, Wavy Gravy is perhaps best known for his announcement from the stage on the third morning of the Woodstock festival, an announcement that was captured for posterity in the documentary "Woodstock," that "What we have in mind is breakfast in bed for 400,000." He also warned the crowd to avoid "bad acid." The members of the Pranksters and the Hog Farm, billed themselves as the "hippie police," or the "please force," and they staffed a free kitchen as well as the bad/trip "freak-out" tent at Woodstock (Ray, 2005, p. 369). They also did what they could to spread news of communes being set up around the country, like the Hog Farm, first located on a mountain overlooking San Fernando Valley, and later, beginning in1967, at Llano, New Mexico (Miller, 1999, p. 42). Overall, the effect of the Pranksters' presence at Woodstock was to bridge the gap between East and West, so that people came to recognize themselves as members of a common alternative youth culture that was national, and even international—as Kesey learned during his brief stay in London at the time.

Further

In 1993, Kesey said of Further, "The old bus, when she got back from Woodstock, her heart was broken. She said, This isn't what I got in the business for—carousing with hippies" (Christensen, 2010, p. 388). So Kesey let the old bus rust-out and rot away in a pond on his property in Oregon. Ironically, by the nineties, artifacts from the Sixties, including those associated with the counterculture, were in great demand by the collectors of such things, including museums. One such museum, ironically the chronicler of a dominant and very conventional narrative of American history, the Smithsonian Museum in Washington, D.C., sent a delegation to Kesey's Oregon farm to talk about making Further an exhibit in the museum—a cultural artifact of the hippies. After being told that it was too late for Further, they were encouraged to look around the farm to see if there was anything else that might serve as a substitute artifact, and after much digging around they came up with an old acid test placard. The delegation from the Smithsonian sent a huge truck out to Oregon to pick up the small placard and take it back to the museum in Washington, D.C., where it was placed in a display next to Archie Bunker's armchair (Christensen, 2010, p. 389). Meanwhile, Kesey had been readying a new Furthur, based on a 1947 International Harvester school bus he bought and painted—like the first Furthur—in psychedelic colors and images. There was a large image of Michelangelo's Adam from the ceiling of the Sistine Chapel reaching out his finger to touch the Cowardly Lion, the Scarecrow whale. Kesey wrote that "Pogo, the comic strip possum, floats above the door in a balloon. The Cowardly Lion, the Scarecrow, the Tin Man, and Toto follow the Yellow Brick road. The Silver Surfer glides along the left rear corner. Diatoms drift into fish and lizards, then into an Egyptian pyramid in a sort of capsule account of evolution" (Christensen, 2010, p. 389). Unfortunately, when representatives of the Smithsonian heard that Kesey was driving around Oregon in a non-original Further which he said he was attempting to pass off on the Smithsonian as the original, they wrote him, "We are not interested in reproductions, facsimiles, simulations, or counterfeits of any description whatsoever." Kesey responded, "Are we dealing with the body or are we dealing with the spirit" (Christensen, 2010, p. 389). For him, Furthur was a symbol, a metaphor for a movement and the spirit of an age. He also began to think that "the bus isn't a thing, it's an event, it doesn't work until it's full of people, and music, and begins to warble and reverberate. It wouldn't be right to turn it into a relic or artifact" (Ibid., p. 390). Kesey was always about the living rather than the dead—and artifacts in a museum were dead. They might as well be in a mausoleum.

But when the Rock and Roll Hall of Fame in Cleveland decided to induct the bus in 1997—asking the Pranksters to drive it to Cleveland—they did not care if it was the original bus or not. This was an appealing offer because it would give Kesey and the Merry Pranksters a chance to come together again, to continue the journey and spirit of the Sixties. Kesey must have known his time was not long—he had been diagnosed with diabetes in 1992—so this would be one final trip. Furthur was to be put on display in the Hall of Fame in a special exhibit of 500 cultural artifacts titled, "I want to Take You Higher: The Psychedelic Era 1965–69."[4] The bus was shipped to Chicago, where Kesey and the Pranksters got onboard for the trip to Cleveland.[5] There the bus would be on display from mid-May through mid-August, when Kesey and the Pranksters would take it on a short trip to Darien Lake to visit Phish before returning to the museum.

Darien Lake Concert

In keeping with their penchant for auto-documentation the trip was released as GrandFurthur Tour Kroniklez, Parts 1 & 2 and made available on a Prankster website.[6] An account of the Darien Lake concert has also has been published in the encyclopedia of everything Phish, *The Phish Companion, 2nd Edition* (2004). Neither provides an adequate account of how the trip to Darien Lake and a Phish concert was arranged, although it certainly was in the interests of Kesey, the Pranksters and Phish to arrange a meeting. For Kesey, it was still important to keep spreading the philosophy and worldview of the counterculture further, and to acknowledge that Phish and its fans were a living link to that counterculture. Kesey, also the prophet of psychedelic drugs for expanding consciousness, was very much in his element at a Phish concert. For Phish, the meeting would be highly symbolic as well, connecting them to living legends of the counterculture just inducted into the Rock and Roll Hall of Fame.

Furthur arrived by 7 pm the night of the show at Darien Lake and was parked in front of the main entrance so that thousands of fans (22,000 showed up that night) saw it as they entered. It was no doubt the object of much discussion—all of which was to remain a mystery for the moment. When Phish began performing its first set and the lot had cleared of people the Pranksters had the Furthur pulled to the backstage area. For the parody on *The Wizard of Oz* they were to put on that evening, Kesey told the Tin Man and the Scarecrow to put on their costumes, and Thor was to prepare them for their roles while the Bozos were to scatter in the audience and act lost. Kesey told everyone, "The theme is we're looking for the lost Bozos." Everyone knew what Kesey was talking about because they had discussed their part in the Phish show on the bus on the way to Darien Lake. It was to be a re-working of a play that Kesey had written in 1993 titled *Twister*.[7] Kesey told the Pranksters: "After the Scarecrow, Tin Man and Frankenstein are onstage, I will cue the Bozos to light the sparklers attached to their hands which will provide the light to guide them back to us. We will have found the Lost Bozos ... and they will come onto the stage and join us. We will be reunited." As always, Kesey played the role of the

"Chief," and in this was the "Wizard of Oz," the one whose words the Pranksters all heeded almost without question. He had the whole thing worked out in his mind already, and the Pranksters' role was to help realize his vision. But Kesey never spoke with formal authority, only with the power of his will and charisma, so the Pranksters went along with this scripting of the event because they trusted him to know how to proceed rather than because they feared what would happen if they did not. Kesey was what the sociologist Max Weber called a "charismatic leader," one who leads not through the authority invested in an office or set of rules and procedures, but through the power of persuasion. This is a style of leadership that was acceptable in the counterculture because it was not rationalized authority over people. People did not have to follow charismatic leaders like Kesey. They chose to do so. Still, there always was a bit of a contradiction between the Pranksters commitment to democratic, communal decision-making and their continuing reliance upon a charismatic leader to make most of the decisions for them.

Kesey's play was about millennial catastrophes about to befall humanity as the year 2000 approached, and although Kesey remarked that the play deals with "end-of-the-millennium angst," he abided by his belief in happy endings. He wrote that his plan was to people the play with a "cast of archetypes ranging from the clearly obvious characters, like the Tin Man and the Scarecrow, to the murky and mysterious, like Elvis and Frankenstein ... scramble them all together in every-bickering banter until they're all crazy at each other's throats, then snap them into sanity with a last-minute tear-jerker twist guaranteed to touch everybody's heart" (Simpson, 2013, p. 2). The play, convoluted as it is, suggests that people can survive the environmental, warring, virus-based apocalypses that loom on the horizon by coming together and helping each other, and that the only thing we really have to fear is fear itself.

It also develops a theme Kesey had come to believe in, influenced no doubt by his experience with LSD. Chaos rules the universe, and rather than try to organize and execute carefully planned responses to crises, Kesey argues for the natural power of chaos in healing society. This translates into an almost libertarian cultural politics—common within the counterculture—in which centralized institutional power and the rule of formal codes and laws is to be replaced with the politics of personal and group freedom, and grassroots change efforts that are locally based. The play borrowed liberally from Grateful Dead, ending with the Wizard singing somewhat revised lyrics to the Dead's *Truckin*: "Lately it's occurred to me/What a glorious trip it still do be, do be, do be, do be!" (Brightman, 1998, 24). The trick was to keep the trip going, as Kesey had, in spite of his declining health. He was diagnosed with diabetes early in the Nineties, and had a stroke shortly after returning to Oregon from Furthur's final journey. To keep the trip going was itself cause for hope, a hope that people could adequately respond to the challenges they faced by continuing to travel further along the road. Beyond what the play had to say, however, which was always a bit confusing given the rambling, sometimes incoherent dialogue, *Twister* broke some theatrical ground by offering the audience a "multimedia, tactile, vertigo-heavy event featuring video productions, lasers, and high-tech sound" (Trager, 1997, p. 229). Kesey was trying to revolutionize theatre, re-encoding its customs by co-opting ritual along with drama (Huffman, 2000, 453).

This technical wizardry made *Twister* a perfect addition to a Phish multi-media concert, and some effort was made by the band to make the play's thematic narrative synch-up with Phish's own mythological narrative of an Oz-like world, *Gamehendge*. That mythological tale, set to music, was about an evil ruler who controls the simple people of Gamehenge by controlling and interpreting their sacred book, "The Helping Friendly Book." Only when the book is returned to the peaceful people of Gamehenge, so that all can read and interpret it themselves, can the people be set free. The song from the Gamehendge "opera" that Phish performed in its second set at Darien Lake that night was *Colonel Forbin's Ascent*, about a revolutionary hero who climbs up a mountain in an attempt to contact Icculus, the god of the sky and the author of the Helping Friendly Book. That song includes the lyrics: "… I warn you that all knowledge seeming innocent and pure/Becomes a deadly weapon in the hands of avarice/and greed." Knowledge, that is, is not neutral. It is always used by power to affect some change; and so it matters very much how knowledge is used, quite apart from any judgment as to its validity. When Phish finished *Colonel Forbin's Ascent*, the band shifted into an improvisational riff as Trey Anastasio, who had been narrating the story, said that Colonel Forbin realizes "that on this particular day he's not going to find the great and knowledgeable Icculus at all, and instead he's going to find Ken/Uncle Sam/Bozo/Easy Kesey standing there ... There he is now."[8]

As the audience erupted in applause and shouts, Kesey strode onto the stage as the Wizard, wearing a black cape and high top hat decorated in stars and stripes, and above the roar of the crowd he emitted several long, powerful "wows ..." as if in despair. "My heart is sorely beset," he went on, "because amongst attendants of these vehicles that are moving through the nation, we have lost a very important part of us. For two years, no one has seen hide nor hair of the Bozos. Where are the booozooooos?" and he feigns crying as he takes off his hat, then breaks into a little dance, while Phish improvise musical support he announces: "What we heard is that they were going to try to make it here to the Phish concert. They decided to come to the Phish concert." He tells a little story about how his brother, the Wizard of Oz, was supposed to be here instead of him, but that he had been arrested in Omaha for "flying too high without any visible signs of support," which was greeted by great laughter among the fans.

Kesey calls on the Scarecrow and the Tinman, costumed like the characters in the movie, *The Wizard of Oz*, to join him on stage and help in the hunt for the Bozos. Then Kesey and Phish shifted the mood of the music from happy and upbeat to dark and scary as Frankenstein walks onto the stage—like the evil Wilson in the Gamehendge saga—as a symbol of the forces of greed and power that want people to feel lost and alone. But the forces of love and family won. As Kesey continued to chant, "Where are the Bozos? Where are the Bozos?", the five Bozos in the crowd begin dancing their way to the stage to join the others. As it was performed that night, the play was about getting lost along the way in life, and about the importance of friends who do not give up on us, who become a second family of lost souls moving as best they can to embrace the light.

Phish continued its second set while the Pranksters exited stage left jumping into Furthur, leaving before the concert ended so they could avoid the traffic jam. In reflecting on the event, Kesey wrote that "music hath powers to soothe the savage beast," a reference to the dark forces represented by Frankenstein, who had moved toward the band in threatening motion only to be "cooled out" by Phish as it segued into their tune *Frankenstein*. Kesey began to think again, as he had thought in the Sixties, that the counterculture could not be built (or re-built) without the power of music, a Dionysian music that would soothe the demons driving humanity toward the apocalypse and usher in an age of love, laughter, and communalism. He would not, however, have the energy or health to contribute as a leader of a Dionysian movement, and so the Darien Lake concert was not necessarily a revival of Kesey's crusade, but rather a passing of the baton of leadership to Phish and the group's fans.

When Kesey returned to Oregon, leaving Furthur at the Rock and Roll Hall of Fame, he suffered a mild stroke that left him unable to use his right arm effectively. In 2001, *The Movie* finally came together as a documentary titled *Magic Trip*. Kesey died following surgery to remove a liver tumor in November 2001. In his last written work, an essay in *Rolling Stone* following the 9/11/01 attacks, he foresaw an apocalyptic time ahead. "It's going to get messy, everyone agrees. It's going to last for years and probably decades ... Nothing will ever be the same." The Real War, he wrote, would not be against the Taliban in Afghanistan, but between the "ancient gutwrenching bonebreaking fleshslashing way things have always been and the timorous and fragile way things might begin to be." His hope remained intact. Although he was aware that the road of peace and love would be a difficult road to follow, he envisioned an "upheaving future" in which humanity would know "honest peace."[9]

Genealogy of the Hippie

Kesey and the Merry Pranksters might be considered the first hippies, and certainly they established a certain long-haired, tie-died, psychedelic style—a style that emerged out of the beat culture of San Francisco. But it was not until the 1967 Summer of Love that the hippie became an identifiable counterculture type in both the U.S. and the U.K. Before then, there were the "beatniks," for a few brief years in the early and mid-1960s. In order to appreciate the enduring power of hippie as an iconic image in American and British popular culture, and within Phish fan culture as well, we must begin with a pre-history of the hippie, a genealogy of the beatnik.

A 1965 British documentary, *Primitive London* by Arnold Miller (now a cult classic), is a good place to start, for it represents a very conforming, conventional, mainstream assessment of several rebellious currents in British youth culture at the time—the mods, rockers, and beatniks.

The beatniks are shown in one of their underground hang-outs where folk musicians perform and hang-out. A young man with shaggy long hair and a guitar performs "John Henry" in his best southern U.S. accent while another young man, doing his best Bob Dylan, accompanies him on harmonica. The style is that of the late folk revival, of an emerging folk rock influenced by the American blues, and by the poetry, passion, and politics of Bob Dylan in 1965 (the year he toured in England). The youth depicted in the documentary are not particularly style conscious (in contrast to another youth sub-culture in London, the mods) and their informal styles serves to make an anti-style statement. The narrator—the voice of the dominant culture—describes the beatniks. First, "their name has something of defeat in it," apparently because it implies that they are beat down, like the beats; and second, "they pride themselves on their nonconformity, but their very revolt serves to emphasize the norms against which they proclaim their rejections." The presumption here seems to be that beatniks' revolt only serves to reinforce the power of the norms of the dominant culture, so that it is a self-defeating revolt by outsiders who will never succeed in overthrowing that dominant culture.

An interviewer talks to several young people in the crowded bar, asking one of them if he works, to which the young man responds, "no, I write poetry." Then, the obligatory question: Do you believe in free love, to which the young man simply responds, "yes." In other interviews it becomes clear that the beatnik youth either do not believe in marriage or define it loosely and openly, as in, "if two people love each other then they're married." When the interviewer asks a group of young women if they would call themselves beatniks, they all reply "no," and when asked if they would marry a beatnik, they laugh and say the same thing. Obviously, they are uncomfortable with being identified as beatniks, suggesting that the label is already beginning to be loaded with negative connotations within popular culture and youth culture. It is a label placed on young people by members of the press, by representatives of the dominant culture, rather than a self-chosen and self-affirmed identity. One young man, asked what his definition of a beatnik is, replies: "I don't like the word me-self. Because if you ask the average person in the street what a beatnik is they'll immediately turn around and say, a person who doesn't wash, doesn't work, just got long filthy hair, and is a parasite on society." When asked if he thinks this is "entirely wrong," the young man replies emphatically, "yes, this is entirely wrong."

A Phish fan I interviewed (whom I will call Angela) told me that she had been a "Phishhead" ever since the late Nineties when she attended a sprawling, suburban, shopping mall high school in Ohio. She went to a Phish concert with her boyfriend at the time and started hanging out with a few other Phishheads at her school. "We were like a clique," she explained. When I asked what other kids in the school called their group, if they called them Phishheads, she said hesitantly and a bit defensively: "They called us hippies. We always corrected them and said we're not hippies, we're Phishheads. But they never stopped calling us hippies. We didn't like being called hippies because we didn't think of ourselves as hippies, like from the Sixties." But they did have much in common with counterculture hippies from that earlier age, expressed through dress or style. Angela noted that before she went to her first Phish concert, she dressed to fit in and took makeup application seriously. After being introduced to Phishhead styles, she no longer wanted to "dress like the kids who bought their clothes at Nordstroms," it all seemed a waste of money and time to be so style conscious and brand-oriented, so she became less about "spending a lot of money to keep up with popular schools fashions."

But in a highly brand oriented, style conscious school culture, that meant Angela and her Phish friends were outsiders, although Angela said they did not really mind that at all. The Phish community and the little cell of Phish fans Angela was part of became a "crew" that went on the road to Phish concerts and that helped support and sustain Angela through an alienating school culture. At the same time, to be a Phishhead or a hippie inevitably was to be an outsider, and in a highly competitive, grade-and-career-oriented high school, hippies were stereotyped as underachieving "stoners." To be called a hippie is to invoke a whole history of negative images in the mainstream or mass media, images that were already being constructed at the time of Woodstock and that have changed and evolved over the decades since. Most Phish fans grew up and were "schooled" by the mass media to accept these images. Whether the hippie is the object of serious ridicule or merely an object of humor, whether the images are from the late 1960s or more recent times, the governing images have remained the same—of lazy dope-heads in tie-die, who are "spaced out," unwilling to work, dirty, and irresponsible, who have no politics other than self-indulgence. Some Phish fans go out of their way to reject the hippie label at least partially because of these controlling images of the hippie constructed by the media industry. They don't want to be associated with an identity that is stigmatized, even within elements of the Phish community.[10]

If there was any "truth" to this controlling image of the "hippie," it is that counterculture youth were and still are predisposed to resist the mind-numbing routines of school life and view them as oppressive, so they sometimes got stoned before or during school to help them get through the day. That in itself does not make them underachievers, however. Many so-called hippies have been quite successful academically, in high school and in college, and gone onto successful careers. But many have also ended up dropping out of high school or college, or getting bad grades, not because they lack the capacity to do well in school, but because they have developed a quite sophisticated critique of the dominant culture's knowledge production. This critique is based upon personal observation of the narrow technical rationality of the curriculum, and their dropping out is a form of resistance to the institutional power relations of schooling within a technocratic society.

In a context in which schooling gets imagined as a panoptic, normalizing form of control over young people, preparing them to be (as Pink Floyd said) "another brick in the wall," many counterculture youth were chronic underachievers in school, or they finished their high school programs in "alternative schools" for drop-out prone kids. In this context they were allowed to express themselves and largely direct their own learning according to their own interests and perceived needs. But most Phish fans, like Angela, did well in high school and went on to college and "responsible" jobs, so it is important to remember that the controlling image of the underachieving hippie is not an accurate representation, but rather an image designed to stigmatize and "Other." That is why it was and is an identity label placed on others by members of a dominant group, and within the mainstream mass media, rather than a self-affirmed identity.

The word "hippie" linguistically connects the counterculture to the word "hip," as in the beat generation phrase "hip cat" or "hep cat" and further back to the West African then African American word "hipi-cat," meaning "one who has his eyes wide open" (Falk, 2005, p. 185). These were terms that took on a positive meaning within "hip" jazz, bebop, and beat cultures. One wanted to be considered hip within these music-based subcultures, because it meant having a heightened sense of style, and a bohemian lifestyle outside "normal" society. Dizzy Gillespie invoked all of these associations in his bebop classic, "Hep Cat's Love Song," and he liked to present himself as the number one hep cat. But the word "hippie" as it was used after the mid-Sixties, rarely took on these positive connotations within the counterculture movement, and as I said, it was not a word these youth typically used to define themselves, unless it was in reaction to being called a hippie, to affirm a stigmatized label.

Controlling images of hippie identity and "lifestyle" already circulated in the mainstream press and mass media at the time of Woodstock, and the media used them like scaffolding to construct the "truth" about Woodstock and what went on there. The commercial mass media is in the business of producing images and narratives, and also selling people images they want to see, and narratives they want hear. At the time of Woodstock, even the respectable, middle class, politically liberal leadership of the *New York Times* presumed its readers wanted one negative image of the counterculture. The *Times'* initial coverage of the festival focused on the trope of the "stoned pilgrim."[11] The article explained to the naïve reader "the argot of the drug scene," arguing that "the Woodstock Music and Art Fair was the focus of that scene in the northeast this weekend." Woodstock is reduced almost entirely in the article to a signifier for the drug scene. A 19-year-old college student was quoted to the effect that "there was so much grass being smoked last night that you could get stoned just sitting there breathing." When participants were asked "How many of the crowd are smoking grass? The almost unanimous response was: "Ninety-nine percent." As for LSD, the article noted that it also was present, "unfortunately for scores of youngsters, and deadly for at least one so far." The article concluded that the whole event and what went on there would be "simply incomprehensible at best, and a flagrant violation of law and morals at worst." When a police officer was asked why there weren't more drug arrests, he said that the jails could not hold all of those breaking the drug laws.

The next day, August 18, the *Times* ran an editorial on the Woodstock festival titled "Nightmare in the Catskills"[12] that began: "The dreams of marijuana and rock music that drew 300,000 [a serious underestimation of attendance] fans and hippies to the Catskills had little more sanity that the impulses that drive the lemmings to march to their deaths in the sea." Rock fans and hippies are reduced to the status of lemmings, all moving in the same conforming direction, heading with the crowd and without thinking toward a cliff. It is unclear from the editorial what the cliff signifies, but one likely meaning left unsaid, is that the cliff is drug addiction and possible death through drug overdose. Given the tone of the *Times'* reporting, we might also view the cliff as a social cliff, associated with the collapse of civilization, law, order and reason. The *Times'* editors argued that parents, teachers, and other adults who helped bring up the young into a society against which they were now rebelling, had to assume "a share of the responsibility for this outrageous episode" in which "pot, acid and other illegal drugs could be freely exchanged." The editors concluded with two rather startling statements on the "redeeming features" of the festival.

One redeeming value was the "genuine kindness" shown by the residents of "overrun" communities near the festival, who helped provide young people with water and sandwiches, along with the doctors and nurses who volunteered their time and efforts. The second redeeming feature of the festival, according to the editorial, was "the fact that the great bulk of the freakish-looking intruders behaved astonishingly well, considering the disappointments and discomforts they encountered." All of this revealed, the editorial concluded, that these young people had "real good underneath their fantastic exteriors," if it could just be put to "some better purpose that the pursuit of LSD." So after being criticized as "freakish-looking intruders," the editorial hints at a narrative of the well-behaved hippie that was to become quite influential in media coverage, and that continues today in the coverage of Phish fans.

From the start, consequently, there were alternative, even competing narratives of the hippie and the rock fan, and of Woodstock as a cultural event, even within the mainstream media. The same *Times'* that ran an editorial on the "Nightmare in the Catskills" could, within another week, on August 24, offer an essay on the "pop" scene that presented a positive narrative of Woodstock, containing many of the tropes or images that would characterize a more progressive narrative of Woodstock—what we might call the Back to the Garden narrative. According to the article[13]: "As the weekend went on, the miracles kept happening—the kindness of the scattered police, the 'food-drop' by an Army helicopter, and flowers from the sky," "faith makes miracles," and so the peace and joy expressed by the participants created "happy results." Here is the very social constructivist notion, radical at the time, that suggests people play an active role in constructing one reality or another, applied in this case to the notion that the Woodstock generation willed a concert of peace and love, and that the fans' "good vibrations" created an event that "impressed the world that watched."

Out of conditions that could have led others to despair, the hippies celebrated "the joy of confirmation." Faith, miracles, and confirmation—these are all religious terms, and the article consequently understood a very secular festival as a religious ritual, at least implicitly. Through the combined power of faith, miracles, and confirmation, the crowd would dance through the mud and rain and the electric failures. They would turn hunger into an opportunity for generosity and sharing. This implicit religious narrative would soon be made explicit in rock operas like *Jesus Christ, Superstar* (1970) and *Godspell* (1971), and in films and recordings such as Arlo Guthrie's "Alice's Restaurant," released as an LP in 1967 and in movie form in 1969, in which a group of rural, country hippies in Massachusetts who take over an old deconsecrated church and make it the festive site of a Thanksgiving feast—a sort of communion. For a public tired of confrontational politics, violence, and war, and longing for a spiritual renewal, this counterculture narrative had a strong appeal. People wanted to believe in something again, to have ideals, as they had when the decade began; and the counterculture was invested with many of the characteristics of the early Christian movement, before it became highly institutionalized and dogmatic.

TIME magazine could see early on that Woodstock was, for good of bad or both, a sign of a major rupture in American culture that would have historical significance. A special editorial in the August 29, 1969 issue of the magazine began:

> The baffling history of mankind is full of obvious turning points and significant events: battles won, treaties signed, rulers elected or deposed, and now, seemingly, planets conquered. Equally important are the great groundswells of popular movements that affect the minds and values of a generation or more, not all of which can be neatly tied to a time and place. Looking back upon the America of the '60s, future historians may well search for the meaning of one such movement. It drew the public's notice on the days and nights of August 15 through 17, 1969, on the 600-acre farm of Max Yasgur in Bethel, N.Y.

In the editorial Woodstock is elevated to the status of other great historical events—battles, treaties, rulers deposed, and even space itself "conquered"—a reference to the Apollo moon landing of the previous month. The event is read as a sign of a shift in thinking and values that is shaping a generation, and that presumably will have a major impact on life in America in the decades ahead.

At their best, as in films like *Easy Rider* and *Alice's Restaurant* (both released in 1969), counterculture youth or hippies were depicted sympathetically as alienated outsiders, drop outs from technocratic society and suburbia, living subsistence-level lives on the road or in communes, and prone to an early death. In *Easy Rider* death comes from the reactionary cultural forces still operating in the South; and in *Alice's Restaurant* it comes in the form of the suicide of a troubled young man. The message is that if hippies go too far outside the boundaries of the normal, they risk their lives, either at their own hands or by reactionary others. This reinforces the controlling image of youth without a future, taken down by "hard" drugs and mental instability, or because they step outside the bounds of acceptable behavior. While the viewer is encouraged to identify with the hippies in both of these Hollywood films, "the hippie" is represented as a risky identity, and the deaths of hippies in the films can be taken symbolically as a moral condemnation or judgment. Still, the generally positive portrayal of "hippies" in *Easy Rider* and *Alice's Restaurant* reflects the year they were made, when it was still possible to take the counterculture seriously as a transformative force for democratic change, although limited by drug abuse and victimized by reactionary cultural forces.

By the late 1970s, the hippie was already becoming a comic character type in Hollywood, revived as someone still living psychically in the Sixties, seemingly unaware that the hippie age is over. This is the imaginary world that the characters Cheech and Chong represent in their series of stoner movies (like *Up in Smoke*, in 1978) where the lovable comic hippies primary goal is to get stoned and stay stoned and not get caught by the police, even when they are driving their old pick-up truck while high. These controlling images indicate just how much the counterculture hippie had become a stock stereotype: not necessarily dangerous (except to his or herself) and often humorous, but also dirty, lazy, sexually promiscuous, and irresponsible.

Die, Hippie, Die[14]

In cartoon form, the 2005 *South Park* episode, *Die, Hippie, Die*, satirically plays with these controlling images but also reinforced them as applied to a band very explicitly modeled after Phish. Not only does the band look like Phish, it is named Fish, and one of the band's fans wears a t-shirt with a psychedelic fish on it. In the show, Cartman operates a pest control business to rid his town of "hippies" who have invaded to attend a local jam band music festival. Cartman observes of the hippies that "they smoke pot, wear crap and smell bad." In the show, hippies "infest" South Park—an analogy to Phish fans as pests—hiding out in basements, smoking dope, laying around, "listening to gay music," and refusing to leave. They have to be driven out of town by Cartman to reestablish the symbolic, normalizing order of South Park and free it from the grip of the plague. The segment begins with Cartman, dressed in pest control gear, appearing at the doorstep of an elderly woman to announce: "Hello, ma'am. I'm working to clean up the neighborhood from parasites. Do you mind if I take a quick look around your house? I'm afraid you may have hippies." He looks in her attic and indeed finds five hippies remarking that "they usually live in colonies," and "these are what we call the giggling stoners, pretty common form of hippie" different from "drum-circle hippies" and "college know-it-all hippies". As the hero who saves South Park from the hippie invasion and infestation, Cartman like Senator McCarthy in the Fifties, is on a mission to drive un-American subversives out of hiding and into the light of day. Cartman announces that hippies may seem harmless at first, but "if you see one hippie, there's probably a whole lot more you're not seeing."

The informed reader may see certain similarities between this South Park episode and the narrative structure of Albert Camus' *The Plague*, in which an infestation of rats carrying the plague, symbols of fascism, wreak havoc in an Algerian city. But here the peace-loving, anti-corporate hippies stand in for the rats in a reversal of cultural politics, as if to say, we don't need to fear fascism as much as a takeover by the counterculture. And in *Die, Hippie, Die*, the perspective is not that of a doctor who sides with the victims of fascism, but rather that of the exterminator "cleaning" the town of a stigmatized social group. Cartman ultimately solves the town's hippie problem (the final solution?) with the aid of a giant drill which he uses to drill through the music festival crowd, killing hundreds of hippies in his path along with the band onstage. If this bloody, cartoon version of a final solution is cynically hip, it feeds a desire to see fantasy acts of aggression committed against stigmatized sub-populations. However, the creators of

South Park, Trey Parker and Matt Stone are satirists first and foremost. Therefore, many young people (including Phish fans) may choose to view this episode as a satire that revolves around the tension between the stereotyped hippie and culture police opposition. In this viewing of the episode, hippies are victims, and Cartman, a witch hunter.

Some viewers will view *Die, Hippie, Die* as an attack on the counterculture of the late Sixties and its continuing legacy in groups and fan communities like Phish. Those viewers who are more cynically satirical in their own thinking, will view it as about poking fun at contemporary hippies and also, simultaneously, about poking fun at the self-proclaimed guardians of public morality. Phish fans seem to love the episode, not only because cartoon Phish characters show up, but also because hippies are the subject of ridicule within some elements of the Phish community as well, who view them as "losers." As one fan wrote in a Phish.net post, "I've seen plenty of these idiotic hippies in my travels. Honestly, I think it's pretty spot on."

Another sub-type of hippie identified by Cartman is "college know-it-all" hippie, one of whom remarks: "We just finished our semester at college. Our professors opened our eyes." What their eyes were opened to was that corporations control everything, so that the shopping mall (for example), is designed by "corporate fatcats to imprison you into a life of servitude." The know-it-all hippie is, consequently, also represented as politically leftist, the product of indoctrination into Marxist "truths" by their college professors. If the giggling stoner hippie is too "wasted" to think about anything too seriously or have a political ideology, the college know-it-all hippie is an intellectual and political activist. On the surface this would appear not to be a bad thing and could even be viewed as a good thing. But within the dominant or normative discourse, the image of the know-it-all college student hippie was a controlling image because it implied that some disaffected youth only felt at home on college campuses rather than the "real" world and might even end up as professors, indoctrinating students into their "radical" anti-corporate, environmental, gender, racial, and sexual politics. This situates the South Park episode within a long history of anti-intellectualism in the U.S. Ironically, some critics of the counterculture had argued that hippies were anti-intellectuals rather than intellectuals, because they rejected rationality and embraced drugs, sex, and mysticism. For example, David McBride has written that "the enthusiasm for both drugs and uninhibited sexuality [among hippies] were part of a broader romanticist impulse encompassing both anti-intellectualism and mysticism" (McBride, 2014, p. 336).

The problem with McBride's argument is, first of all, that it reduces a complex social movement and youthful sub-culture to drugs and "uninhibited" sexuality. Not everyone who identified as a hippie also identified with the counterculture, nor abused drugs, nor let their sexual impulses guide them. One could even be a sexually abstinent and abstaining hippie—something that the Hare Krishna movement taught. Second, McBride assumes that the romanticist movement in American culture—which he correctly links to the counterculture—is anti-intellectual. Romanticism has been a literary, artistic, and interpretive movement in American culture that has had a great influence in the university and among intellectuals of all types. It is just that it is an intellectualism that critiques what Roszak called "objective consciousness." Adherence to a narrow-defined rationality is not what distinguishes the democratic intellectual, but rather an interest in the diverse ways people make sense of the world, including the imaginative and the "magical." Both the representation of hippies as anti-intellectuals ruled by passions and mysticism, and conversely as overly-intellectual "nerds," misrepresent and oversimplify counterculture youth. In fact, the relationship between college students and professors has been important in the making of a counterculture and making sure that the counterculture has had some politics to it. But in the increasingly anti-intellectual and even reactionary political climate since the 1970s, the intellectual has been made an object of ridicule, and so the "know-it-all" hippie is ridiculed not for being anti-intellectual or ignorant, but precisely because she or he is an intellectual.

While the South Park episode, *Die Hippie, Die*, parodied and satirized, it also reinforced and reproduced controlling images of counterculture youth, which academics have often taken for granted in writing about the counterculture. For example, Marley Brant, an authority on the history of the rock music festival, identifies as sub-types of the hippie the "hand-to-mouth" hippie and the "weekend warrior" hippie.

The former type could not afford to go to the Monterey Pop Festival or Woodstock. Like the beatniks and bohemians of an earlier time, they formed their own "insular society predominately in communes or small hovels off the street" (2008, p. 10). These were the street hippies, young kids who had left their small town existences to move to San Francisco, Seattle, and other big cities with growing counterculture communities. As a college student at the University of Washington in Seattle, I remember that after the 1967 Summer of Love in San Francisco, young hippies or "flower children" began flocking to the University District and hanging out all day panhandling on the "Ave," the main drag of the district. Many of these youth were unable or unwilling to work, and without any means of subsistence, many of them ended up abusing drugs available on the street. These young people were often the brunt of jokes by university students who walked by them on the sidewalks, and some considered them a public nuisance. But they were part of the emerging counterculture community in the U-District in Seattle, and many students and passers-by helped them out with spare change when they could. The flower children were, in this regard, treated a bit like the Buddhist monks whose subsistence depended on passers-by offering them food. In fact, the Hare Krishna movement did end up feeding many of these young people for free, and a number of them went on to join that movement. The poverty of the flower children, after all, was chosen and based on an ideological rejection of most work in the "establishment." They also, as Brant notes, viewed organized music festivals as "another type of organized exploitation of their new-found music and brotherhood" (Brant, 2010, p. 10). As for the "weekend warriors," Brant recognizes in them the beginning of a movement away from radical cultural politics and movements to the counterculture as a fashion statement—a movement that would only accelerate in the Seventies. Weekend warriors, she writes, were mostly middle class teenagers and college students "who dressed in pretty clothes and grew their hair long to be in style rather than from a need to rebel." They often professed a commitment to peace and love, but weren't about to shed their comfortable lifestyles in the suburbs or risk advancing their career options (Ibid.).

What makes these controlling images, whether they are presented within popular culture or academic texts, is that they treat the hippie as Other. As such, the hippie reinforces and privileges the norms and moral codes of the dominant culture by providing a ready image of the ab-normal, the object of both a condemning and a humorous gaze. There is just enough good sense in controlling images to make them have a wide public appeal; and elements of the counterculture "lifestyle" are not above being made the object of humor. But the humor in controlling images is based on laughing at the Other, and making fun of "Otherness" so that normality is reaffirmed and reestablished as the norm. In contrast, counter images represent the hippie as offering a serious and even potentially transformative critique of the dominant social order and its cultural norms and mores. Counter images and narratives may (and often do) criticize various types of the hippie, but not in the service of reinforcing established cultural norms, mores, and power relations. Rather, criticisms are meant to help counterculture movements recognize and overcome some of their contradictions and limitations so that they can more fully realize their democratic progressive potential. Of course, some texts contain a mix of controlling and counter images, and I do not mean to suggest that we can neatly divided representations into two opposing groups, one that supports the dominant order and one that supports transformative social change. It is important to recognize, however, that no images and narratives are ever politically neutral, and that culture is a site of conflict over how movements and identities get represented and how their stories get told.

Phishheads have grown up with these various images and narratives of the hippie and the counterculture, and real conflicts exist within the Phish community between those who respond to hippies through moral condemnation, tolerance, and active support. A fan discussion thread on Phish.net in 2010, titled "Does the Phish crowd now hate hippies?" offers revealing examples of each of these responses.[15] The fan who started the thread posed this question because he had heard more and more talk at Phish concerts about "wookies" and (almost a synonym) "dirty hippies." Wookie jokes abounded. At one concert, according to the fan, a young man with dread locks (the usual sign of a wookie) lay on the ground and asked, "what am I?" He answered his own question: "a passed out wookie," a reference to drug and/or alcohol abuse. All of this concerned the fan who started the thread and so he wondered whether hippies were still welcome in the Phish community or whether fans had become overly judgmental and exclusionary. That touched off a long discussion. One woman posted that it was possible to be a hippie and not a "dirty hippie," and that she enjoyed being a "free spirit" herself, believing that being a hippie was more about attitude than "the look," and that it did not mean you were "dirty." In response, another fan accused the woman of being over-sensitive and shared one of his own favorite hippie jokes: "How do you keep a hippie out of your business? Put a Help Wanted sign in the window." Another fan confessed to being a hippie who followed the Grateful Dead before they broke up, where 90% of the fans at a concert were hippies—even in the 90s. At Phish concerts, especially of late, he felt like an outsider, although he claimed to not be bothered when people "single 'us' out and laugh." After all, as a hippie at Dead shows he used to laugh at the "local preppy well dressed dude with his girlfriend." This fan seemed to have learned from the experience of being "Othered" in the Phish community that in fact it is not good to make fun of anyone or relegate them to an object of ridicule, even "preppies." So he accepts being laughed at not because it doesn't bother him, but rather because he too has made jokes at the expense of the Other.

One fan posted that most Phish fans would not consider themselves hippies because they "could care less about their environmental impact, social injustices or equality." His mom, he wrote, had been a hippie back in the Sixties, but most hippies "turned into Yuppies." In the Sixties, hippies had a purpose—"free love and ending the Vietnam war,"—but according to this fan the purpose has been lost, and hippies today are all style ("wearing ratty looking clothes and some sandals") with no radical politics. Another fan took a "why can't we all get along" attitude, and called on others to accept all Phish fans as brothers and sisters regardless of appearance. In response, a fan often identified as a "wookie" lamented that it had become "socially unacceptable" to dress or look like a "wookie" or "whatever you want to call us." Another posted that what he hated most was the "snide comments and stink eyes" directed at so-called hippies at Phish concerts. "I'm not saying we can't all get along or that it even matters, but at what point did 'the hippie' stop being a huge part of the scene and why the distain?" Clearly, a guiding principle within Phish culture is what we might call the principle of getting along, but this fan suggested it was hypocritical to talk about getting along when some fans obviously did not welcome hippies and wookies. As another fan noted, the result has been a decline in their numbers at Phish concerts and an increase in the number of "really clean, sharp looking people." Sometimes these are referred to as "regular" fans. As a descriptor, "regular" implies "normal," whereas the hippie and the wookie are relegated to the status of the ir-regular and the ab-normal.

Phish has contributed its own images of the hippie in the band's song *Prep School Hippie*, which is also known as *Trust Fund Baby*. The song was performed on five occasions in 1985 and 1986, and then dropped from the band's repertoire apparently because it was a song that made fun of and insulted some of the band's fans.[16] The song pokes fun of both Grateful Dead hippies and prep school hippies. The narrator can't decide between a "Big ten kegger at the frat/Or watching Jerry [Garcia] shake his fat." Meanwhile, his mind drifts back to the trust fund that awaits him when he turns 21. Is this a controlling image or a counter image of the hippie? In one sense it represents a very insightful critique and is not about representing the viewpoint of the dominant culture and social order. Indeed, prep school and trust fund hippies are representatives of that culture and order. In this sense, the song is counter hegemonic, that is, critical of dominant social groups and power blocs. But it also may be considered a controlling image in that it insults and stereotypes a distinct group of upper middle class fans, similar to the "weekend warrior" hippie, a type who goes to a Grateful Dead or Phish concert just to dress up in tie-dye, get wasted and party, then return to their privileged prep school existences. Not everyone who goes to a prep school or has a trust fund waiting for them is that shallow and uncritical. In fact, this is the class background of the Phish band members and of those who come from privileged backgrounds but are able to critique their own privilege—like Pete Seeger did.

Counterculture to Culture Industry

By the early Seventies, the counterculture was already in decline as the idealism, unconventionality, and revolutionary spirit of the Sixties began to give way to increasing cynicism and conservatism. Indeed, some would say that the crowning achievement of the counterculture was Woodstock, and that after Woodstock it was all decline. The Altamont Speedway Free Concert, held less than six months after Woodstock in December, 1969, is often represented as the anti-Woodstock. One fan was killed in a violent confrontation with Hell's Angels, cars were broken into and property stolen, and there was much property damage to the concert venue. Soon thereafter, on May 4, 1970, National Guard troops opened fire on unarmed "hippie" anti-war protesters at Kent State University, killing four and wounding nine. The politically conscious and activist wing of the counterculture movement would respond with student strikes and protests; but the back of the movement had been broken, along with its spirit. Crosby, Stills, Nash, and Young would voice some of the counterculture despair in their popular song, *Four Dead in Ohio*. In the face of "Armies of Nixon coming," the song suggested that "we're finally on our own." Counterculture youth could not look to political leadership or "middle Americans" to do anything but repress and oppress them, and try to make them "fit in." If counterculture youth were on their own culturally, it was because it was becoming clearer all the time that the "establishment" would tolerate only so much dissent, and that the revolution was not going to happen.

The counterculture also began to collapse under the weight of its own success. Rock fusion music provides a good case in point. The rock fusion music performed at Woodstock was an expression of the counterculture. It was critical of the dominant order and normative culture, and it was political and even revolutionary in its intentions. When the Jefferson Airplane, the ultimate hippie band from San Francisco, performed "Volunteers," when Joan Baez connected the counterculture to the folk revival with "We Shall Overcome" and "Joe Hill," when Country Joe and the Fish performed their darkly humorous "Vietnam" song, and when Jimi Hendrix closed the concert with a powerfully subversive playing of the national anthem, the major popular music artists of the time saw themselves as representing, or speaking and singing for, the counterculture and the cultural revolution the counterculture was leading. At the same time, there were deep contradictions in the increasing commercialization of the kind of music performed at Woodstock. For example, the Jefferson Airplane's "Volunteers," that included the lines, "Look what's happening out in the streets/Got a revolution," was the title of a song and an album that was a best seller for RCA in 1969. While the song's lyrics can be taken seriously, the album cover cannot. Members of the band dressed in crazy, clownish costumes with liner notes which poked fun at revolutionaries. Taken together this provides a normalizing interpretation of the music that supports the notion that counterculture heroes are more pranksters than revolutionaries, more Kesey than Guevara. Pranksters operate within space provided by the liberal order; jesters dance in the throne room under the auspices of royalty.

The hope had been that rock artists could maintain their countercultural politics, along with creative control of their music, but once they began recording for major record labels and performing at rock concerts and festivals they became business ventures. In some ways, Bob Dylan had been the model for this type of highly-commercial artist who does not compromise his art and his message. But as rock artists became part of what Joni Mitchell called the "star-making machinery," it became increasingly difficult to sustain this hope, at least without a lot of compromises. The Jefferson Airplane, which had started out playing psychedelic, experimental, and improvisational rock in small venues in San Francisco, tried to reassert itself as an authentic voice of the counterculture by morphing into Jefferson Starship and recording the concept album, *Blows Against the Empire* (1970), which had no cuts that might conceivably be released as top 40 singles. The album celebrates the coming together of the counterculture in opposition to "Uncle Samuel," and the stealing of a starship so that the counterculture can search for a new home in the sky. While the album was presented as a further development of counterculture themes, the counterculture is clearly represented as "on the run," looking for a home of its own outside a dominant culture that was not only resistant to change but striking back.

There was a shift in thinking within the counterculture that was reflected in the growth of the Back to the Land and rural commune movement of this time. For all of its artistic creativity and musical and thematic complexity as a concept album, *Blows Against the Empire* did not sell anything close to the group's *Volunteers* album, with its more commercial appeal and ready singles. So the band went through another metamorphosis by the mid-Seventies to become a purveyor of romantic, smooth-sounding single hits, like *Miracles* on the 1975 album *Red Octupus*. By the eighties they had morphed again to Starship but now as an "urban rock" band, with hits such as *We Built This City* in 1985.

Conclusion

Other Sixties rock fusion artists were somewhat better at holding onto their political and cultural commitments and not "selling out" so completely. The Grateful Dead is the obvious example of a band that performed at Woodstock that did not sell out, and its loyal fan base of Deadhead hippies would keep the counterculture alive at Dead concerts over the next three decades, until Jerry Garcia's death in 1995. Some of the counterculture ethos of the Dead concerts was taken up again in 2009, by resurrecting the name Further one more time, this time not to describe the bus itself, but rather a band that carried on some of the spirit of the bus, formed by former Dead members Bob Weir and Phil Lesh. For Phish and the community of Phishheads, the Grateful Dead is the model for a financially successful rock band that did not sell out to the media industry and the star-making machinery, and that maintained the spirit of the counterculture in conservative, even reactionary, times. This entailed a commitment to controlling the production and distribution of their own music.

Aside from the music of the counterculture, the media industry would prove capable of assimilating counterculture images, styles, and events (including Woodstock) into a system of commodity consumption. As Bruce Pollock, a social historian of the counterculture has observed, counterculture youth "wanted to overcome repression in the name of id .... But desire unleashed is not necessarily desire fulfilled; it is more likely to be desire entertained" (Pollock, 2009, p. xviii). Conservative social critics like Allan Bloom were wrong to assume that a release of Dionysian desire was the primary aim of the counterculture, or that Dionysian desire is merely about self-indulgence and narcissism. The desublimation of desire (as Marcuse recognized) could be revolutionary, especially when it is tied to a critique of disciplinary and repressive apparatuses of control. Furthermore, the aims of the counterculture were much broader than the desublimation of desire. They included commitments to communitarianism (that found expression in the commune movement and a belief in sharing wealth and the land), to social justice and human freedom (that found expression in opposition to race, class, gender, and sexual "Othering"), to the re-spiritualization of the life-world (that entailed the re-appropriation and valuing of indigenous epistemologies and ways of being in the world). Pollock writes that: "Alongside the claims of the counterculture for ecstasy, there coexisted a craving for a sort of public love, a communal self-determination, access to one or another kind of God" (2009, p. xix).

The radical democratic spirit of the counterculture and Woodstock has not entirely dissipated in the decades—as witnessed by the Phish fan's comments about having a "Woodstock moment." However, that spirit has lost much, if not all, of its transformative utopianism. Certainly, there always have been problems with utopian movements, since utopian ideals of communalism, personal freedom, and radical love are transcendent constructs that have to be applied in a real world, and reality always fails to live up to utopian promises. That should not however, be an excuse for abandoning utopianism; to no longer practice imagining a world of peace, love and communalism. But that seems to have been the societal response. Sometime in the Seventies people began to stop believing in the utopian, transformative vision of the counterculture, becoming more cynical, pragmatic, and more willing to "sell out" (Wicke, 1987).

In 1971, The Jefferson Airplane still held onto the dream but voiced in *When the Earth Moves Again*, a new cynicism about the revolution happening. The earth would move again, sometime. But for now, the counterculture is represented like the Jewish people fleeing Egypt, but not so lucky: "The Red Sea closes over you when you least expect it to." An important reason for the success of anti-utopianism is the overwhelming mass media offensive that covered the complex territory of counterculture youth subjectivities with a cartooned image of the "hippie." Although some young people wore the badge of hippie proudly, most often the term was used to refer to images of narcissistic, irresponsible, lazy, dirty, drugged-out, and immoral young people. It should be of no surprise, consequently, that the hippie label is rejected by so many Phish fans, and rightfully so most of the time. Yet, many Phish and Grateful Dead fans, along with Boomers whose identities were forged out of the late Sixties counterculture, still seek out "Woodstock moments," and they hold out hope that the earth will move again.

Notes

1. Here the author is suggesting a continuation of this mode of analysis through the work of Gilles Deleuze and Felix Guattari in *Anti-Oedipus* and through Guattari to Anthony Negri who continued this work with Michael Hardt in the triology Empire, Multitude, Commonwealth.
2. Garcia & Kesey—NBC Tom Synder 1981 5–7 (part 1) https://www.youtube.com/watch?v=2Egz_ex3d_s. Retrieved 8.15.2014
3. Sterling Lord. When Kerouac met Kesey: The two counterculture heroes, one representing the Beat '50s and one the psychedelic '60s, had a lot less in common than you might expect. *The American Scholar*, 2011 (Autumn), available online at http://theamericanscholar.org/when-kerouac-met-kesey/#.U-5iNlZtfUQ. Retrieved 8.15.14
4. Kesey to Give Bus to Museum, *Seattle Times*, April 22, 1997. http://community.seattletimes.nwsource.com/archive/?date=19970422&slug=2535208. Retrieved 8.13.14
5. Ken Kesey to Deliver Magic Bus. *The Spokane Spokesman-Review*, April 22, 1997, 7.
6. http://intrepidtrips.com/grandfurthur/kroniklez2ndleg.html
7. *Twister: A Ritual Reality in Three Quarters Plus Overtime if Necessary* was first performed on July 21, 1993, at the National Guard Armory in Eugene, Oregon following a Grateful Dead show in town, so that Deadheads—the heirs of the

counterculture—could come. http://phish.net/song/merry-pranksters-jam/history Merry Pranksters Jam. Retrieved June 5, 2013
8. Authors description of the Darien Lake show draws from several sources, including: Merry Pranksters Jam. http://phish.net/song/merry-pranksters-jam/history. Retrieved June 5, 2013; *The Phish Companion, 2nd Edition*, 594; and Colonel Forbin's Ascent into Merry Pranksters Jam—Phish, Youtube. https://www.youtube.com/watch?v=CvqUqsqBqnE. Retrieved 8.18.14
9. Ken Kesey. The Real War. http://www.democraticunderground.com/discuss/duboard.php?az=view_all&address=389x3339003. Retrieved 8.19.14
10. See the discussion thread: Does the Phish crowd now hate hippies? http://backup.phish.net/demos/sticky.php?thread=1285768789. Retrieved June 4, 2013.
11. The *New York Times* article headline for August 17, 1969, "Bethel Pilgrims Smoke 'Grass'" and Some Take LSD to "Groove." http://graphics8.nytimes.com/packages/pdf/topics/Woodstock/19690817Groove.pdf
12. The full article can be found here: http://graphics8.nytimes.com/packages/pdf/topics/Woodstock/1969WoodstockEditorial.pdf
13. http://graphics8.nytimes.com/packages/pdf/topics/Woodstock/19690817GoodThings.pdf. Retrieved 15.7.14.
14. Episode 902—Die Hippie, Die. http://www.spscriptorium.com/Season9/E902script.htm. Retrieved 8.22.14
15. See the thread here: Does the Phish Crowd Now Hate Hippies? 1010 thread on Phish.net. http://forum.phish.net/forum/show/1285768789. Retrieved 12.11.13
16. Prep School Hippie: http://phish.net/song/prep-school-hippie/history

References

Brant, M. (2008). *Join together! Forty years of the rock festival*. New York: Hal Leonard.
Brightman, C. (1998). *Sweet chaos: The Grateful Dead's American adventure*. New York: Simon & Schuster.
Butler, J. (1990). *Gender trouble*. New York: Routledge.
Caouette, N. (2014). Beats by the Bay: Sixties San Francisco music and the development of a contemporary tourism industry. In Tara Brabazon (Ed.), *City imagining: Regeneration, renewal and decay* (pp. 183–194). New York: Springer.
Cavallo, D. (2001). *A fiction of the past: The sixties in American history*. New York: St. Martin's Press.
Christensen, M. (2010). *Ken Kesey, Acid Christ: Ken Kesey, LSD, and the politics of ecstasy*. Tucson, AZ: Schaffner Press.
Cross, C. R. (2005). *Room full of mirrors: A biography of Jimi Hendrix*. New York: Hyperion.
Dettmar, K. (2006). *Is rock dead?* New York: Routledge.
Dodgson, R. (2013). *It's all a kind of magic: The young Ken Kesey*. Madison: University of Wisconsin Press.

Falk, G., & Falk, U. (2005). *Youth culture and the generation gap.* New York: Algora Publishing.
Foucault. M. (1970). *The order of things.* London: Tavistock.
Foucault, M. (1997). *Ethics: Subjectivity and truth.* New York: Penguin Press.
Freedman. J. (2000). *The temple of culture: Assimilation and anti-semitism in literary Anglo-America.* Oxford, UK: Oxford University Press.
Gehr, R. (1998). *The Phish book.* New York: Random House.
Gitlin, T. (1993). *The sixties: Years of hope, days of rage.* New York: Bantam.
Huffman, B. (2000). Twister: Ken Kesey's multimedia theatre. *Modern Drama, 43* (Fall).
Johnston, D. (2007). The electric Nietzsche deadhead test: *The birth of tragedy* and the psychedelic experience. In Steven Gimbel (Ed.), *The Grateful Dead and philosophy.* Chicago, IL: Carus Publishing.
Kramer, M. (2013). *The republic of rock: Music and citizenship in the sixties counterculture.* Oxford, UK: Oxford University Press.
Littleproud, B., & Hague, J. (2009). *Woodstock—Peace, music, and memories.* Lola, WI: Krause Publications.
McBride, D. (2014). Counterculture. In William Deverell & Greg Hise (Eds.), A companion to Los Angeles. Malden, MA: Blackwell.
Miller, T. (1999). *The 60s communes: Hippies and beyond.* Syracuse, NY: Syracuse University Press.
Mills, K. (2006). *The road story and the rebel: Moving through film, fiction, and television.* Carbondale: Southern Illinois University Press.
Nietzsche, F. (1969). *Ecce homo.* New York: Vintage.
Nietzsche, F. (1995). *The birth of tragedy and the spirit of music.* New York: Dover Publications.
Pollock, B. (2009). *By the time we got to woodstock: The great rock 'n' roll revolution of 1969.* Milwaukee, WI: Backbeat Books.
Ray, T. (2005). Wavy Gravy (Hugh Romney) (1936-). In William Lawlor (Ed.), *Beat culture: Lifestyles, icons, and impact* (p. 369). Santa Barbara, CA: ABC-CLIO.
Reynolds, S. (2009). *Woodstock revisited: 50 far out, groovy, peace-loving, flashback-inducing stories from those who were there.* Avon, MA: Adams Media.
Roszak, T. (1995). *The making of a counter culture: Reflections on the technocratic society and its youthful opposition.* Berkeley: University of California Press.
Schumacher, E. F. (1993). *Small is beautiful: A study of economics as if people mattered.* New York: Vintage Books.
Simpson, P. (2013). *A brief guide to Oz: 75 years going over the rainbow* (chapter 4, p. 2). London: Constable & Robinson Ltd.
Trager, O. (1997). *The American book of the dead: The definitive Grateful Dead encyclopedia.* New York: Simon & Schuster.
Wicke, P. (1987). *Rock music: Culture, aesthetics and sociology.* Cambridge, UK: Cambridge University Press.
Wolfe, T. (2008). *The electric kool-aid acid test.* New York: Picador.

Chapter Four

(Not) Dead Phish

In *The Phish Book* (1998), authored collectively by Richard Gehr and Phish band members, who speak in both their individual and their collective voices, the collective voice observes that Phish had covered several Dead songs in its first years on the road, but it dropped them "to avoid the onus of being pigeonholed as yet another Dead cover band" (Gehr & Phish, p. 16). One thing this indicates is that even when the Grateful Dead were still performing on the road, they were being "covered" by bands who sought to perform the Dead, to be a reasonable facsimile of an original. These Dead cover bands are very much part of local and regional Deadhead cultural gatherings. The other thing that this passage reveals is that Phish felt the need to not cover many Dead songs, in order to establish their own identity and their own material. The collective voice of Phish represents the Dead as "enmeshed in the working-class politics and emotions of another era entirely." The Dead were "products of the West Coast's beat/hippie scene," while Phish "came of age on the East Coast during the postpunk eighties" (ibid.). This rhetorical distancing from the Dead continues as Trey remarks that he went to his first Dead show with a neighbor, "and I didn't even pay attention," "didn't get it," that it was "boring." Then he took some blotter acid and suddenly "I got it" (ibid.). This rhetorical distancing is also something the fans engage in. Phish fans may make fun of Deadheads, and vice versa. For the Grateful Dead's 50th anniversary concert in Chicago in the summer of 2015, the band asked Trey Anastasio to join the group, filling the spot left empty by Jerry Garcia, which immediately causes an internet stir among Dead fans, for whom no one could replace Garcia, and certainly not a member of a jam band that was not of the same caliber as the Dead.

All this posturing and rhetorical distancing by both Phish and Grateful Dead fans, of course, is in the face of very obvious similarities. Mike Gordon of Phish acknowledges that Phish shares with the Dead a fundamental belief that music is not primarily about encouraging young people to "revolt against societal institutions in an overtly political way" (Gehr & Phish, p. 119), but rather to "break radical new ground" in small ways, encouraging people to "celebrate life in all its diversity" (ibid.). This is a bit ambiguous, but it does speak of music and concert experiences as small spaces where young people can learn to celebrate diversity of class, race, gender, sexual identity, religious identification, and other markers of difference. The irony is that fan communities may be taken as examples of relatively homogeneous White, middle class communities, so that they allowed the democratic possibilities of this celebration of diversity to go under-developed.

The Grateful Dead and Phish also share common roots in the psychedelic movement in counterculture rock in the late Sixties, which also means viewing the psychedelic experience as spiritual, communal, transcendence. This association with psychedelia and a drug culture, of course, created major problems for both bands at a certain point. Jon Fishman notes, "I've met a lot of kids who follow us because of the Grateful Dead thing, which seemed to get out of control toward the end, as though the pests had destroyed the cornfield" (Gehr & Phish, p. 112). That could just as well be said of the Phish community before the band went on a hiatus in August 2004, after the debacle of the festival at Coventry, Vermont. The "pests" (which Fishman also refers to as "parasites") are, presumably, the drug dealers, and the fans (and band members) who are so wasted on drugs that they couldn't participate in the "purpose" of the show.

That purpose, according to Fishman, is to provide "something people don't get elsewhere ... a communal nerve that makes people want to live a life that parallels what we do musically" (ibid.). Here Fishman makes a subtle and important distinction. On the one hand, the Dead provide an example of a youth culture organized around coming together as a community, to experience their "communal nerve," (ibid.) to imagine a life that mirrors in some ways the music the band performs. Fishman never elaborates, but the band's music creates a communal space for democratic spontaneity, difference, and flow. In these ways the purpose of the band's music is radically unsettling and subversive of the normative culture. But Fishman's comments also point to something else, the tendency of the drug culture of Dead and Phish concerts and festivals to get out of hand, to become debilitating, and to stifle creativity. In both cases, the increasing drug use among fans was mirrored in the bands, and so both reinforced one another in a vicious cycle.

When Jerry Garcia died and the Dead stopped touring in 1995, many Deadheads migrated to the Phish community, which grew in size accordingly. The Dead did it first, and showed that it was possible to build counterculture communities around music, in which people came to listen to the music to be sure, but also, and perhaps more importantly, to participate in a collective, communal, improvisational, spiritual engagement with the moment. That is why, as I have already said, the concert and festival venue became so important by the 1980s in the effort to maintain elements of a counterculture resistance to normalization in an age when White middle class youth were being reintegrated into their positions of privilege in the dominant culture, their resistances to the Oedipal family, schooling for docility, and the social and technical relations of the workplace, largely over.

The counterculture of the Sixties was constructed around praxis, in which young people engaged in action to change the world, and to live the vision of a better, more humane, less-alienating way of "being in the world" (Heidegger & Stambaugh, 1996, p. 50), to use Heidegger's phrase. By the Eighties, American youth had entered a postmodern world in which image is reality—images that could be appropriated, commodified, and sold back to youth through the culture industry, and in the process stripped of a democratic cultural politics. Identification with the Dead (and Phish) communities was performed—a style of dress, a way of talking that had cultural capital within the community. The weekend counterculture was the result. Put on your tie-dye and beads for weekend Dead concerts, then go back to their "normal" and normalizing performance of self for the rest of the week. In such a postmodern form, it is hard to see how the Deadhead counterculture represented a significant threat to the normalizing, disciplinary, and surveillance powers of the family, the school, and the workplace. Of course, the possibility always exists that in performing a Deadhead or Phishhead identity, fans also identify with a radical critique of American society and resist "fitting in" in ways that cannot be fully contained and incorporated. Consequently, to speak of the incorporation of Dead-based counterculture within the "way things are," is not exactly accurate. It is not a question of being incorporated or not incorporated, but rather a question of the ways in which youth culture is part of a dynamic contested social order, in which incorporation of dissent is never complete.

In writing about the Dead and Deadhead culture, I draw upon some of the literature from "Dead studies"—an academic movement that takes Deadhead culture seriously as an important cultural phenomenon with broad implications for youth studies, the study of "outsider" communities, and concerts and festivals as ritual performances in which young people are inducted into community and identity. Dead studies is a truly multidisciplinary field of study, with contributors from philosophy, social science, the humanities, and even religious studies. A recent bibliography of scholarship in Dead studies included entries for well over four thousand individual articles, books, papers, and other written work relating to the Grateful Dead (Dodd, 2005, p. xv), which makes the band perhaps "the most studied band in the academy" (Meriwether, 2012, p. 25). There are also a few personal accounts of life on the road with the Dead, including Phil Lesh's (2005) influential autobiography, *Searching for the Sound: My Life with the Grateful Dead*.[1] I mention Dead studies not only because I intend to draw upon some of this scholarship to situate the Dead and Deadhead youth culture within a cultural history or genealogy of the counterculture, but also because it points to something important: the links between Deadhead culture and the culture of liberal arts colleges and universities. On such campuses, a bit of bohemianism and unconventionality is allowed and even respected, along with dialogue, inquiry, and academic freedom. Granted, this liberal ideal never has been realized fully, and even to the extent that it has been, it always ends up constructing the university as an insulated, elitist space, guarding its borders with the "real world." But it has provided a relatively safe space for dissent and unconventional thinking and lifestyles, and for this reason the counterculture has found a home in liberal arts colleges and universities. The liberal arts university becomes a protected and safe space for middle-class youth, one in which they are given the opportunity to explore alternative lifestyles and worldviews as part of their identity formation, and so Deadhead culture thrived in the liberal arts academy. They found there a habitus, a way of life that was generally consistent with the values of Deadhead culture.

The town of Berkeley, California, and the University of California at Berkeley played a formative role in this regard, and the town of Berkeley came to define the Deadhead image. Members of the Dead lived in and around Berkeley and were much influenced by the progressive cultural politics and lifestyles of the town (Schinder & Schwartz, p. 329). The Berkeley street scene also provided elements that would become incorporated into Deadhead concerts, including a craft economy that existed outside of the highly-commercialized youth culture market. The street scene that stretched out along Telegraph Avenue near the Sather Gage entrance to campus included, according to the *Insider's Guide to Berkeley and the East Bay* (Fowler, 2002) "vendors selling beaded and silver jewelry, handpainted silk scarves,... and tie-dyed T-shirts ready for a

---

[1] Also See: Parish & Layden (2003), *Home Before Daylight: My Life on the Road with the Grateful Dead*, and Scully & Dalton (2001), *Living With the Dead: Twenty Years on the Bus with Garcia and the Grateful Dead*.

Grateful Dead concert" (p. 158). The Guide cautions tourists that many students and former students who hang out on Telegraph Avenue "look like holdouts from the Grateful Dead era, with their long swirly skirts in natural fabrics, lots of bangled jewelry, head scarves, long hair, and scruffy beards" (ibid.). As this is the judgment of a tourists' guide, it may be interpreted as a compliment, for it is the voice of the dominant culture speaking, "otherizing" and exoticizing those who refuse to be assimilated into the normal. For all of these reasons, the counterculture found a protected or safe space in the liberal arts academy and in communities like Berkeley, and so the counterculture developed its own "organic intellectuals"—writers, teachers, and activists who represented the larger Deadhead community and helped articulate its values through Dead studies.

Because the Grateful Dead was forged out of the Sixties counterculture and came to represent that counterculture throughout the following decades, the group and the Deadhead community illuminate what some social historians have called the "Long Sixties," the continuation of Sixties progressive cultural forms in a conservative age. Rob Weir (2014) writes that the Long Sixties is a cultural construct that serves as a window through which it is possible to "view the changing meaning of the Sixties as they played out in *fin de siècle* America," that is, America at the end of a century and also the end of an era characterized by progressive cultural politics (p. 137). That era was, of course, already ending in the late 1960s with the election of Richard Nixon on a "law and order" platform, and the growth of a backlash movement (with strong appeal among a White working class in decline) against the gains of women and African Americans and in defense of "traditional family values." In education, Ira Shor (1992) has shown how this "conservative restoration" was expressed in the nation's schools and colleges by a ratcheting-up of disciplinary power over student (and teacher) bodies, along with a regimentation and predetermination of the curriculum (tied to standardized testing) that effectively exerted technical control over the content of the curriculum and its "delivery" (Shor, 1992, p. 159).

At the highest levels of the state, as expressed in the Reagan Administration's report on the "crisis" in public education, *A Nation*

At Risk (Gardner et al., 1983), there was a call for higher standards, which also meant eliminating the "progressive" courses that appealed to young people and that had found their way into the high school and college curriculum in the Sixties and Seventies, like Afro-American history, the history of jazz and rock, women in literature, sexuality and sex education, and so on. The call was for a "back to basics" curriculum of math and literacy skills, with efforts made to target instruction for socioeconomically disadvantaged youth to remediate their skill "deficits." In many ways, the conservative restoration in American education was a response to a perceived permissiveness in the Sixties, which was in turn blamed for encouraging students to "experiment" with alternative lifestyles, use drugs, disrespect their teachers and other authority figures, and demand that the curriculum be tailored to their desires. The culture of the Sixties, Shor observes, "posed immediate and long-term threats to authority ... [putting] business, schooling, and the government on the defensive" (Shor, 1992, p. 3). One of the results was a return to "law and order" in the classroom, a more tightly controlled and predetermined curriculum in the nation's schools, and more surveillance of students and teachers. The answer to the problem of alienated youth was thus represented in terms of a desire left unfulfilled in a "permissive" culture, a desire for more adult discipline and authority.

Hollywood films about high school in the 1980s, like *Stand and Deliver* (1988) and *Lean on Me* (1989), incorporated the new conservative restoration ideology, with stern authority figures represented as heroes saving troubled urban (i.e., Black and Latina/o) youth. In contradistinction to this disciplinary and surveillance narrative, which assumed young people really wanted to be disciplined and were alienated and disaffected because they did not have authority figures that set the rules, was the narrative represented in *The Breakfast Club* (1985), in which youthful alienation from the schooling process is related to an institutional process—a set of beliefs, rituals, and structures—that is only interested in conformity and obedience. What the "breakfast club" in Saturday detention learns is that they have to turn more to each other to meet their needs, and to youthful subcultures of identity like heavy metal and punk. But this more sympathetic treatment of youthful angst and alienation was out of synch with the new conservative ideology of the 1980s that was hegemonic in state-sponsored educational reform. The real effect of this increase in disciplinary and surveillance power over youth was to drive them out of school completely, or to increase their subtle forms of in-school resistance to that power exercised over them, as an oppressive power—or to carve out a liminal space of their own, to form a community of young people looking for something more than the dominant culture had to offer them, a community like the Deadheads.

While the Deadhead phenomenon was a response to changing times after the collapse of the 60s counterculture and the rise of cultural conservatism and a heightened concern for the surveillance and policing of youth, these changes affected working class and suburban youth somewhat differently. Suburban youth in high school and college, still maintained their relative privilege, although they felt more pressure to get ahead in an increasingly competitive job market for college graduates, and this meant learning to study hard for good grades and test scores on standardized tests, thinking competitively, and conforming to get ahead. The character of Alex in the popular Eighties situation comedy, *Family Ties*, was the new Eighties model for middle class, suburban teens (at least if they were male): rebel against your Sixties counterculture parents as out of touch, and still believing all those outdated Sixties beliefs about love, peace, cooperation, community, and equality. Young people in suburban schools and on college campuses were no longer protesting. Instead, they were learning to develop a competitive edge in the professional-managerial labor market, learning how to market themselves by performing the self. The image no longer hid anything "real" or authentic behind it. In a perfect postmodern way, the image was the reality, or so these young people were led to believe. If they projected and performed the right image, nothing could hold them back. The same basis image for successful youth is represented in *The Cosby Show*, one tailored to middle-class Black youth in a supposedly "raceless" society where nothing held them back but their own failure to think in terms of professional career building and establishing their own middle-class respectable families after college. David Byrne, of The Talking Heads, wrote about growing up in suburban Baltimore: "My generation makes fun of the suburb and the shopping malls, the TV commercials and the sitcoms that we grew up with." But the suburbs were also hard to shake from their collective consciousness. "Though we couldn't wait to get out of these places they were something like comfort food for us." Furthermore, growing up in middle-class suburbia forever marked you apart from an urban cultural elite. "We are not and can never be the urban sophisticates ... and neither are we rural specimens—stoic, self-sufficient, and relaxed." Byrne concludes that these suburbs "still push emotional buttons for us: they're both attractive and deeply disturbing" (David Byrne. *Bicycle Diaries*. New York: Viking, 2009. p. 9).

It is these "emotional buttons" and the psychic disturbances they produce that are expressed in The Talking Heads' album, *Remain in Light*. For a significant number of suburban youth, these suburban disturbances led them to the Dead community of suburban misfits and outsiders. But unlike many of the counterculture youth of the Sixties, they did not seek to drop out of the suburbs entirely or live on utopian communes. For many, the Dead community provided a space they did not need to inhabit continuously. They could continue their educations in the "system," and learn to fit in enough to get into top tier colleges and universities, and then pursue careers in the "system." Then, on weekends, or for special "gatherings of the tribe," they could become Deadheads—for a day or a week. Of course, some did drop out of the suburbs entirely, and out of the suburban dream of success, to follow the Dead on the road, often dropping out of college or even high school to live a life at the margins of economic subsistence, surviving by selling drugs or food or bumper stickers, and often made the subject of derision by other fans and the popular press. But the narrative of counterculture youth on the road was also compelling because it organically connected Deadheads to the beat culture Kerouac depicted in *On the Road*. To be "on the road" is to be, at least for a time, outside the normal, and thus "free" in a certain way.

The Deadhead community was constructed out of exiles from suburbia—the new middle class—but also out of exiles from the working class. By the 1970s, one identifiable youthful subculture in high schools across the U.S. was the hippie, and it was embraced more by working class than suburban middle-class youth. Middle-class kids were alienated conformists in high school, at least for the most part. They might put on tie-dyed garb for weekend Dead concerts, but they could not afford to perform a hippie identity within school if they wanted to get ahead. The working class hippie subculture, on the other hand, literally wore their hippie identities to school—through their style of fashion, their long hair, their refusal to compete for grades and with each other, and were resistant to the oppressive authority relations of schooling. Like the "Lads," a group of working class boys that Paul Willis studied in the U.K. in the early Seventies, many working class youth in the U.S. refused to take school too seriously. It was boring, meaningless work, that was preparing them for alienated adult labor. Working class youth who identified with the hippie or Deadhead image lived for other values. In the late Sixties through mid-Seventies, many of these alienated, working class youth ended up in progressive "alternative" schools and classroom programs designed to keep them in school until they could graduate. These programs were designed to be "homey," with overstuffed couches, rugs for students to stretch out on the floor, and teachers who related on an informal and personal level to students (See Silberman). But by the late Seventies, most of these programs were gone, and many of the youth they served were pushed out of school before they could pass the new state-mandated standardized graduation tests and graduate. The Deadhead community consequently did bring youth together across class lines, based on a common alienation from a schooling process, although those who could afford to attend Dead concerts were more likely to be the college kids, the weekend hippies. Certainly, the Dead's own cultural politics were very much about representing the working people, the common folk—something that comes across most clearly and forcefully on their 1970 album, *Working Class Hero*.

By the Seventies, the cultural politics of the counterculture had become less Marxist-oriented, and the Deadhead culture that survived in the coming decades had largely left behind notions of social transformation and settled for the promise of occasional transcendent spiritual experiences and subversive play. If all of these concerns with spiritual experiences of connectedness and transcendence, and with Dionysian play, can be found in the counterculture of the late Sixties Woodstock

Nation, they were mixed much more at that time with an overtly political engagement in grassroots social movements of protest and the re-imagining of democratic public life. Little of this radical cultural politics remained by the late Seventies, and substance began to give way to image—the image of Sixties style without much substance, without much behind the image. But this postmodern concern for image without substance has never been complete. The appeal of the authentic, the real, is strong in youth culture, and fans often exhibit a capacity to distinguish between both fans and bands who are "real," and those who are just performing or selling an image. Indeed, this helps explain the appeal of the Dead among "real" Deadheads. The band took itself and its music seriously, and its message was about not "selling out," not "fitting in," not transforming yourself into a marketable image with no substance behind it. And what is "substance?" By substance I mean a set of beliefs and values, a discourse, on personal and (relatedly) social transformation. Whether this substance takes the form of political activism designed to challenge hegemony, as it often did in the Sixties, or takes the form of movements aimed at challenging and transcending dominant ways of thinking and being-in-the-world consistent with the building of a more democratic, equitable, and just age, perhaps matters less than this substantive engagement in transformative change.

The Dead, and much of the counterculture from the late Sixties onward, were substantive in this latter sense, of being committed to changes in human consciousness that would encourage new ways of living together, and this in turn would affect broader democratic changes.

The lyrics to their songs were not for the most part overtly political, and the Dead may be associated with a retreat from the era of protest rock in the Sixties. But their songs did speak to the importance of equity, freedom, and inclusive communities—and also engaged in a critique of what was wrong with "normal," mainstream, suburban American life—its consumerism, its idolatry of money and social status, its banality, and the psychological disruptions and alienation it created in youth. If the Dead held out hope, it was a limited hope, as expressed in one of the group's standards, "A Touch of Gray," the first stanza of which ends with the proclamation, "I will get by, I will survive," and the last stanza with "we will get by, we will survive." I, individually in my life, and we, as a community, a tribe of Deadheads, will get by and survive, and in Dead culture the two were always understood to be one and the same. Fans survived living in a conservative age because they had a tribe, a community, with which they identified, and because they periodically could gather with the tribe. What was special and unique about the Dead was the community that mobilized around them and that sustained itself (and the group) for four decades.

The Grateful Dead core group, as it existed in 1965, included Jerry Garcia, Phil Lesh, Bob Weir, Bill Kreutzmann, and Ron "Pigpen" McKerman of the Merry Pranksters. Other musicians joined in for a time, and the band went through a number of incarnations over the course of its "long strange trip." But the band always remained true to its roots, and these roots were planted firmly in the soil of San Francisco's counterculture and the city's bohemian scene. Nicholas Merriweather observes that "from the outset, the band was considered a vital part of the counterculture of the sixties in general and of the Haight-Ashbury in particular," (Meriwether, p. 33) and McNally argues that the bohemian tradition, "one shared by everyone in the Grateful Dead—was linked also to ... their identity as San Franciscans" (McNally, p. 11). The city had been settled by merchants and industrialists to be sure, but also by outcasts from the east and mid-west, seeking a new beginning, a space where they would not feel marginalized, in which, according to McNally, a "wayward tolerance for freedom" prevailed (McNally, p. 11). All of the Dead members "came out" of and in this rich cultural environment. I use the term "came out" in a dual sense. On the one hand it references the environment from which youth come, their habitus of origins. This habitus was San Francisco bohemianism, which provided a supportive environment for youth to "invent" themselves anew, but also within the history of bohemianism and the latest manifestation of the tradition—the beats who in the early sixties were still very much part of the San Francisco scene. A second meaning of the term "came out" takes its meaning from the modern LGBTQ movement, and refers to coming out as an affirmation of an open, gay identity; so that we can say that the band and the Deadheads came out in San Francisco as identified with a marginalized group, a counterculture of affirmation and community outside of, or alongside of, "straight" society.

Garcia's schooling and upbringing provide an example of something that was going on at the time more generally in the making of a counterculture. Dennis McNally, provided a description of Garcia's education and upbringing in *A Long Strange Trip: The Inside History of the Grateful Dead* (2002), that helps illuminate some of the ways in which the counterculture of the Sixties was forged out of resistance to the power relations of schooling. Garcia came from a "cultured" middle-class family in the Mission District of San Francisco. His parents were both musicians—his mother a student of opera, his father a performer in a swing band—and they seem to have been supportive of their son's creative and artistic inclinations, often in opposition to school officials who understood his endeavors in terms of "behavior problems." Suffice it to say, Garcia got into "trouble" because he was unwilling and/or unable to adapt to the school's regimented routines and authority relations, along with the Eurocentrism of a curriculum that made Mexican Americans and their cultural contributions almost invisible. His resistance took the form of minor infractions: smoking in the boys' room, fighting, and cutting classes (McNally, 2002, p. 15). But Garcia was not always a "bad" student. There were occasions when teachers encouraged, motivated and served as role models for him; and at these times he excelled. As early as the third grade a young teacher encouraged his artistic pursuits, and according to McNally, "soon he felt not only a blossoming identity as an artist, but also a general sense of being different from most other people" (McNally, 2002, p. 9). In 1955, when he was in the eighth grade, his parents finally succeeded in getting him enrolled in a Fast Learner Program at Menlo Oaks school, which was progressive in its pedagogy and curriculum. His new teacher was a true bohemian artist, who arrived at school on his motorcycle or in his MG, and who was regularly in trouble with the school administration because "he threw open the class to discussion and introduced them to D.H. Lawrence and George Orwell" (McNally, 2002, p. 12). This was the kind of education, and teacher, that inspired Garcia and kept him in the system. But he was never a "good" (i.e., conforming and submissive) student, as defined by the normative culture of schooling.

The only school he would be proud of attending was a college, the California School of Fine Arts (later the San Francisco Art Institute), which was a bridge between the academy and an emerging counterculture in the city. There Garcia got a good counterculture education. One faculty member told Garcia that "he and his friends were the real Beat Generation, and sent them down the hill to North Beach and its coffeehouses to, as Garcia said later, 'pick up my basic beatnik chops,' listening to Lawrence Ferlinghetti read at the Coexistence Bagel Shop" McNally, 2002, p. 14. Along the way Garcia was to stop at City Lights Bookstore to pick up Jack Kerouac's *On the Road*, a book that would change his life forever and lead him later to meet Neil Cassady—Dean Moriarty in the novel, along with Ken Kesey; this would change everything. But before that Garcia began to experience his life as out of control—a chaos that seemed to be throwing him forward, as if in a storm, without him being able to do anything to wrest some order out of the chaos. He served a brief stint in the Army thinking that what he needed might be more control and discipline, but he kept going AWOL and was discharged. According to McNally, it was music that saved Garcia, so that "as his life slid further out of control, music became the only stabilizing force available to him" (McNally, 2002, p. 15).

It was bluegrass and the blues, particularly. The folk revival of the early 60s gave him both a musical direction and a political purpose. He decided he would learn the music of bluegrass folk masters and emulated their style, and then perform within the bluegrass folk circuit to serious audiences. He would not write his own music but rather committed himself to the discipline of mastering and performing the American bluegrass tradition on guitar and banjo. As Dylan was working his way into the Greenwich Village folk scene in the early Sixties, Garcia was doing the same in San Francisco, and he quickly got to know future collaborators Paul Kantner, Jorma Kaukonen, Joan Baez, and David Crosby (see McNally, 2002, p. 49). By the Spring of 1963 Garcia had formed his own bluegrass group, the Hart Valley Drifters, with himself on banjo, and they performed at the Monterey Folk Festival in the amateur division, winning Best Group. Dylan had also been at Monterey that year and managed to alienate Garcia (the folk purist) by writing and performing his own songs outside the folk canon

(McNally, 2002, p. 50). That canon and the structure of the music in it, provided Garcia with a bounded world and the kind of discipline he felt he needed to keep the chaos at bay. His was not the politically conscious and active folk revival of Seeger, Guthrie, Dylan, Baez, Belafonte and others—the explicitly pro-civil rights, anti-war folk revival. Rather it was the folk revival of a pure folk music with apolitical lyrics. At this time in his life and arguably later, as McNally observes, "Garcia was an apolitical artist, certainly pro-civil rights and intuitively liberal, but at heart concerned only with music and its performance" (McNally, 2002, p. 32).

It is highly ironic that as Garcia began to forge a counterculture identity in the bohemian context of San Francisco, he also began to feel by 1964 that his commitment to performing the bluegrass canon might mean he had to leave San Francisco, where the music scene was experimental and avant garde and there was increasingly little space left for purists like himself to perform. Before making any decisions about his future, Garcia decided to take a trip to the home of bluegrass and blues music, the American South. Garcia and a friend drove through the Jim Crow South in a type of grand tour of the roots of bluegrass music, recreating some of the atmosphere of Kerouac's *On the Road* in the process. This was Freedom Summer, when White middle-class college students from the North were being mobilized to register Black voters in the South under the leadership of the SNCC created by African American college students. That summer of 1964, three male college students working for Freedom Summer (two White and one African American) were murdered by the Klan in Mississippi. These were the children of the folk revival, imbued with a strong sense of working for social justice; but as I said, this was not Garcia's folk revival, and so he passed through the South without seeing much of the battle. But Garcia would remember the South as "creepy." McNally writes, "His first sight of 'colored' drinking fountains and bathrooms was shocking, and grew no easier with repetition. He realized he was naïve in his San Francisco tolerance, and the South's legacy of bigotry and fear overwhelmed him" (McNally, 2002, p. 71). If this was the home of "pure" bluegrass and blues music, it was a "creepy" home, and this led him to question these folk traditions, and this in turn reinforced his sense of needing to return to San Francisco, as "the positive place" (McNally, 2002, p. 37) within which he could find himself as a musician and dare to let out the creative, if also somewhat chaotic, forces within him. In some ways this was a return to what was comfortable and familiar, but it was also a return to a San Francisco music and youth culture scene in the process of transformation.

Both sides of the new counterculture—associated with political activism and with heightened consciousness—were organizing themselves in San Francisco in the fall of 1964. The politically activist counterculture was organizing around what would become known as the Berkeley Free Speech Movement, which demanded that the administration lift its ban on campus protests and other activities and asserted students' rights to free speech on campus. The protest movement became most well-known, perhaps, to the public when students were arrested for carrying placards imprints with banned obscene words. That seemed a relatively trivial example of free speech, but it did provide a vehicle for mobilizing thousands of young people and teaching them the tactics of protest—tactics some of the students had learned in protests against Jim Crow laws in the South. It also helped establish by mid-decade the principle that the academy was a free space, a space of protest and tolerance for unpopular opinions, that would inform student protests throughout the rest of the Sixties. Mario Savio, a student leader in the Free Speech movement said, rather ominously, "There's a time when the operation of the machine becomes so odious, makes you so sick at heart, that you can't take part ... and you've got to make it stop" (quoted in McNally, 2002, pp. 74–75). Joan Baez sang "Blowing in the Wind" at a student protest rally as a thousand students entered and occupied the administration building. Future Grateful Dead members couldn't help but be affected by what increasingly looked like a revolution going on around them. Hunter drove a delivery van to Berkeley each day and was a bit concerned about the "too violent-feeling" he sensed among some protesters, but he sympathized with their cause. Weir looked to Savio as role model for a new kind of leader. Garcia was fascinated and sided with the student protesters, but McNally concludes that "he was apolitical, distrusting demonstrations on principle" (McNally, 2002, pp. 74–75).

The counterculture's two segments—the political activists and the consciousness-raising spiritualists—held together because they saw each other as ultimately sharing a critique of the dominant culture and pursuing the same goal, that is, bringing about a cultural revolution in America. But they had very different notions as to how this was to be brought about, and what exactly the alternative would look like. Garcia and the Dead, from the beginning, represented themselves as about consciousness-raising, not direct political activism, and consciousness-raising meant "acid rock." Hunter had first been introduced to LSD when he had made extra money, along with Kesey, by participating in what would turn out to be CIA-sponsored experiments with psychedelic drugs at a Veterans Administration hospital. Hunter told others, some of whom would become the Dead, about his use of the drug and they were, according to McNally, "transfixed." Hunter would write that most people are enmeshed in "the most GODAWFUL prison of concrete and veins and consciousness," while he felt "PURE WHITE SPIRIT" pouring from each vein ... By my faith if this be insanity, then for the love of God permit me to remain insane" (quoted in McNally, 2002, pp. 42–43). Hunter had become a true believer in the new religion of LSD, and his sense that young people had to walk through a door, become "experienced," transform their own way of thinking, was a prerequisite in order to be capable of transforming the culture. Garcia took LSD for the first time in April 1965, and he seemed to confirm Hunter's sense of the promise of the drug as revolutionary. His experience with LSD had completely disillusioned him about the capacity to maintain control and predetermination of outcomes in a chaotic, moving universe. Garcia concluded that his vision of music as a bluegrass folk artist had been too small. According to McNally: "Now that the strictures of his own limited imagination were gone, he would enter a more fluid realm, where anything was possible. This included something never before contemplated: rock music with intellectual content" (McNally, 2002, p. 81). He began to listen to Dylan, but not the early folk Dylan, rather the latest plugged-in Dylan with its deeply poetic lyrics that spoke of human longing, perseverance, love and loss—all the human emotions explored by Blues artists, but with a new sound. Dylan's *Bringing It All Back Home* album was for Garcia a breakthrough, and it took him to a new places in his own work, and confirmed his sense of a home in San Francisco.

Out of the fusion of these new sounds and movements in the Bay area, the core Dead group began to coalesce in the late spring of 1965, first as the Warlocks, including Lesh, Weir, Garcia, and Pigpen, playing what they called electric blues-based music, mostly of their own creation. The group quickly established itself as part of the mushrooming counterculture community in San Francisco. Gone was Garcia's narrow commitment to bluegrass music and in its place was a commitment to learning and playing the blues. The band members worked with the best. They connected with John Coltrane, who had performed in San Francisco jazz clubs in the late 1950s and had a significant influence on the emerging San Francisco counterculture scene and sound (McNally, 2002, p. 91). Lesh would be particularly influenced by Coltrane's breakthrough albums: *My Favorite Things* (1961), *Africa/Brass* (1961), and *A Love Supreme* (1966)—all albums that broke from his bebop roots, introduced improvisation (with all band members playing off each other's improvisations), and created a fusion jazz sound that crossed all ethic and racial boundaries. McNally observes of Coltrane: "His influence on the Warlocks was omnipresent and permanent. Interestingly, that same fall Coltrane experienced LSD and came to the very similar conclusions about it as had the Warlocks" (McNally, 2002, p. 92).

In 1965, the Warlocks changed their name to the Grateful Dead. This name change served as an homage to their newly discovered spiritual and psychedelic insights. It also suggested an awareness of the passage of one's life as that of being thrown toward death—an existential theme—and an acknowledgment of the inseparability of life and death—a religious theme associated with the Mexican Day of the Dead festivities. Finally, the name Grateful Dead suggests a humorous approach to life. Since we're all living skeletons and life is short, we might as well laugh at it all and join in the dance of life. Some have been critical of this humorous approach to life and death. Nadya Zimmerman, for example, writes: "The Grateful Dead pacified what had been a serious religious fascination with death in medieval times and transformed it into a light, even comical, take on death with the playful skeletons on their album covers and poster art ..." (Zimmerman, p. 202) I think this misrepresents the medieval European attitude toward dead—which was often treated as the subject of humor—and also misrepresents the complexity of the Grateful Dead name as a sign in the Dead's system of signs.

The Grateful Dead name was also, as I said, psychedelic, in that it suggested something about the LSD experience of seeing one's life as existing in a moving moment of time. It was almost inevitable that the Grateful Dead would be introduced to Ken Kesey the prophet of a counterculture mobilized through the LSD experience and the organizer of the "acid tests" being conducted throughout the Bay area by 1965. It would be accurate I believe to say that the Dead were enthusiastic believers in the LSD revolution from the first time they took the drug. Garcia would later report that "this is what I've been looking for. You know I've been a seeker all along, and this is at least part of what it was I was looking for and maybe even more" (quoted in McNally, 2002, p. 80). According to McNally, "LSD's impact on all of them would be positive and liberating. Garcia most of all." While the bluegrass banjo he was leaving behind was all about discipline and control, "the combination of LSD and electricity [creating 'plugged-in' music] would set them free." Whereas previously their vision of music was "too small," now the limits or blinders on their own thinking about, and experience of, music was of a "fluid realm, where anything was possible" (McNally, 2002, p. 81). McNally quotes Kesey to the effect that: "We always thought of the Grateful Dead as being the engine that was driving the spaceship we were traveling on" (quoted in McNally, 2002, p. 112). That metaphoric spaceship was, like that of the Jefferson Starship, on a journey of discovery, of leaving the familiar behind and taking fans into new realms of knowledge and experience. The metaphor of the starship on a mission of discovery was developed in the Sixties by the television show *Star Trek*, and in a more psychedelic form by Stanley Kubrick's *2001: A Space Odyssey*. The concert was an experience of self-discovery for the Deadhead community, of discovering who they were as an identity group and also who they were individually, and this occurred within what McNally refers to as an "extreme psychedelic environment" (McNally, 2002, p. 107). LSD was to be the key that opened the door to another, visionary world; and consequently it would be inaccurate to view the psychedelic movement in the counterculture as merely about getting "high." At the same time, the early promise of the psychedelic experience began to diminish over time, like all drug-induced experiences. Near the end of the Dead's long strange road trip, in the early nineties, the promise of the Sixties psychedelic revolution had given way to the reality of drug abuse and addiction, and Garcia's musical vision began to dim, even if that vision was never extinguished.

The acid tests and the psychedelic movement in the counterculture did provide a model for counterculture youth to come together at concerts and festivals, where the having of "IT" experiences was a ritual performance. Overall, as the cultural anthropologist Victor Turner would have said, the Dead concert was a ritual of separation from the dominant culture, and of liminality or learning to live on the margins of that culture, as an insider/outsider who crosses borders. For Turner, liminality characterized a state where individuals felt in limbo, between two worlds. They could no longer identity with the dominant culture they had been raised in (Friedlander, p. 535; Daly, p. 70). Although at some point, Turner argued, most young people become reincorporated into the dominant culture (in which case liminality is a phase), he also treated it as fundamentally changing young people, particularly if it was associated with recurrent pilgrimates. "Liminars," as Turner referred to them, learn to live between two worlds and to bring each into dialectic relation. In *The Ritual Process* first published in 1969, Turner argued that young liminars bring structure into relation with anarchy or anti-structure, and in this way allows the dominant culture to stay open to change, revision, even transformation. "Liminal entities," he wrote, "are neither here nor there; they are betwixt and between the positions assigned and arrayed by law, custom, convention, and ceremonial." As "ambiguous and indeterminate" subjects, they help open up a field of freedom. ...(p. 95) (quoted in Daly, pp. 70–71). In *Dramas, Fields, and Metaphors*, Turner wrote of the capacity of liminality to overcome the bondage to the past, to open a gap in culture: "... the possibility exists of standing aside not only from one's own social position but from all social positions and of formulating a potentially unlimited series of alternative social arrangements" (pp. 13–14). Among these alternatives, are formulations of a community of equals, or communitas, along with an interpretive discourse that allows the liminar to deconstruct the commonsense of the dominant culture. Furthermore, according to Turner, communitas and critique become ritualized within alternative youth cultures.

In Dead studies, Natalie Dollar has used Turner's theory to argue that Dead concerts functioned as rituals of "liminality toward communitas—as well as for acquiring a body of cultural and interpretive logic" (Dollar, p. 53). Of course, a ritual can only function to promote and sustain liminality if it is not overly fixed in its form, but rather ritualizes the dialectic between structure and anti-structure. Dollar uses as an example of such rituals the Deadhead phenomenon of "spinning," or dancing to concert music in ways that weave together solidarity, wholeness, and structure with improvisation, openness, and individual difference (Dollar, p. 59). The spinners were followers of the Dead on tour, most of whom identified with the so-called "Rainbow Family" of counterculture youth seeking spiritual enlightenment. At both Dead and Phish concerts, of course, fans do not sit still but rather dance to their own inner beat and rhythm. Spinners would spin around and around at Dead concerts like the Whirling Dervishes in the Sufi Muslim faith, with the aim of achieving an altered or heightened consciousness, and often without the use of psychedelic drugs. Phil Lesh has written of the spinners that they manifested "the same sort of spontaneous consensus seen in flocks of birds, school of fish, or clusters of galaxies." They were ordered by the same natural laws that governed "evolution of weather patterns, or the turbulence in a rising column of smoke" (quoted in Kaler, pp. 144–145). In the Phish community, this phenomenon—of order emerging out of chaos and then dissolving again—is also ritualized when fans with glow sticks on an arena floor are seen from those above. Sometimes, the lights seem to move in waves across the arena floor, and at other times create spontaneous patterns. This is part of the concert experience of a communitas that is not and cannot be preplanned. If it is a ritual of freedom and democracy it is one that cannot be fixed but must be performed anew at each concert.

The counterculture grew, developed, and sustained itself through these concert rituals and experiences, which is why it could never be sustained by individual fans listening to studio-recorded albums distributed by the media industry. As Nicholas Merriweather notes: "All Deadheads would agree that live performances were the raison d'etre of the band ... the goal was to court the muse of collective improvisation and see where she led; this lay at the heart of why fans went to show after show, year after year" (Merriwether, p. 31). This meant that the performance of music on the stage was subordinated to, or on accurately integrated with, a larger performance of community at the concerts. As Nancy Reist has noted, "hundreds of Dead Heads show up for concerts but never actually go inside. Instead, they congregate in the parking lot, forming a Grateful Dead community that follows the band on the road, rather like a traveling band of gypsies" (Reist, p. 183). They became the real fabric of Deadhead culture, as much or more than the band. This helps explain why the Dead never could be interpreted primarily in terms of the music they recorded or even performed "live" at concerts, in sharp contrast to groups like the Beatles and the Rolling Stones.

The lyrics to Dead songs nevertheless are not to be dismissed as merely background music—a kind of counterculture Musak—without real substance or significance, merely an accompaniment for a psychedelic concert experience. Through their songs the Dead engaged in educating their fans in a distinctive worldview. Although Robert Hunter and John Barlow, the primarily lyricists for the Dead, stuck to writing lyrics, and the Dead band members stuck to creating the music, it was always a case of the lyrics reflecting a collective worldview rather than that of the lyricists alone. And the lyrics were meant to be heard, rather than submerged behind a wall of electrified sound. Basically, Dead songs (not surprisingly) echoed Beat themes and tropes, which were themselves heavily indebted to the Buddhism of Allan Watts, a Buddhism translated and adapted to Beat culture by Kerouac and Ginsberg, and the Buddhism of Herman Hesse's *Siddhartha*, a 1922 novel that was popularized by the counterculture in the Sixties. The central themes of this Buddhism are expressed well in the song "Eyes of the World." Enlightenment is associated with waking "to find out that you are the eyes of the world," and that awareness is associated with a radical deconstruction of the object-subject, external-internal, reason-feeling binary oppositions that were entrenched in the modern mindset and set the standard for what is "normal" thinking. Interestingly, the counterculture's radical re-thinking of the world in the late sixties, that laid the groundwork for a new vision of democratic public life, was already being belittled by the early Seventies in the mainstream media, including the rock press.

In a 1974 *Rolling Stone* review of the Grateful Dead's *Wake of the Flood* (1973) album, the critic points out that many of the album's cuts, including "Eyes of the World," were written in an earlier time, up to five years ago, and that they came across as examples of "blissed-out hippie-dippyness ... Jonathan Seagull would blush" (Miller). Jonathan Seagull is a reference to the national best-selling novella of the early Seventies, *Jonathan Livingston Seagull*, by Richard Bach, about a seagull who learns to soar above other seagulls to a "higher plane of consciousness," in which he learns that he can use his mind to project himself anywhere in the universe. This was certainly an example of taking counterculture themes and dumbing-them-down to a mass audience, but the book's critics took it to reveal the shallowness of the counterculture, its out-of-date appeals, and its inability to live in or deal with the "real" world. Ironically, this appraisal of the Dead by the popular rock press, ignoring them for the most part and dismissing them as relics of the Sixties hippie era when they did acknowledge their existence, only solidified among the Dead and the community forming around them that they were liminal outsiders, strangers in a strange land, preservers of a sacred wisdom. The emergence by the mid-Seventies of a Deadhead community, with its own rituals of induction and its own belief systems, must be viewed as a reaction formation against this treatment of exclusion and even stigmatization. The Dead were invisible and absent in the mainstream, and so they would not try to curry favor with the mainstream but rather go their own way building their own community of fellow-travelers. This type of community has similarities, as Dollar observes, to the early Christian tradition of "seeing the community of believers as one body, with each of the parts having its separate role." This tradition has a genealogy that includes the ecstatic Christian communities addressed in Paul's Corinthian correspondence (1 *Corinthians* 12:4–31). Of course, this genealogy in more recent times also includes ecstatic "cult" communities, and the counterculture was not immune to the appeal of such communities. But cult communities, such as the Manson Family Ranch, Heaven's Gate's Earthship, and Jonestown—all of which attracted counterculture youth and grown-ups who had dropped out of the normal, were distinguished from democratic communities like the Deadheads in important ways. Instead of open concert and festival gatherings, such cult communities gathered in compounds, taking followers out of their formal lives and replacing it with an insular, totalizing vision of the world, led by an all-controlling leader or spiritual guru (http://architizer.com/blog/cult-itecture/ Katherine Wisniewski. Cult-itecture: The Compounds of Intentional Communities. Posted 11/18/2013/, retrieved 3/22/2015). Garcia, Lesh, and other members of the Dead, all refused to play the role of the guru, even if some of their fans wanted them to do so. They insisted that the community would maximize individual freedoms, that there be no dogma, and that the truths communicated in Dead songs be about freeing people and teaching them to distrust gurus and all authority figures.

The distrust of authority and disciplinary power within the Deadhead community was grounded in a politics of difference that took two related but distinctively different forms in the counterculture: an individualistic politics of difference that sought to maximize individual self-determination, and a radical democratic politics of difference that situated the specificity and uniqueness of each individual within the multiplicity of social movements and struggles that define it. Laclau and Mouffe, in their influential mid-Eighties theoretical call for a new "radical democracy" organized around difference rather than uniformity, argued that "the project for a radical and plural democracy, in a primary sense, is nothing other than the struggle for a maximum autonomization of spheres" (HSS, p. 167). The radical specificity of each individual, as a human subject, consequently demands that the democratic revolution and the egalitarian imaginary be advanced by a dispersal of power. At the same time, they are quite clear, as many counterculture youth in the Sixties were, that given the freedom of self-determination, people would understand themselves within a complex web of relationships and social movements for change. There could be no unified democratic revolution, only a revolution of specific social movements, addressing individual differences, who had in common only this: a belief in maximizing and preserving the freedom of all to be different, and for this they would have to come together at times. This is obviously a very powerful ethic of radical democracy that had enormous appeal in the counterculture since it was consistent with an American ethos of individualism and self-determination, although it arguably provides little "glue" for holding a community or social movements for change together.

It is now time to confront again, in this genealogy of the Deadhead community, the central tension that ran throughout the counterculture—from the beats on. That tension (we might even say contradiction) had to do with a divergent politics of self-determination. Everyone who identified with the counterculture supported the principal of the maximization of freedom as a primary democratic project, and believed that a radical decentering of cultural power to the grassroots was needed, so that individuals, groups, and movements could determine themselves rather than be determined by the disciplinary powers and authority relations of the patriarchal family, educational institutions, the workplace, and the sphere of consumption. We might say that all of the resistances against disciplinary power and authority were anti-Oedipal. As Deleuze and Guattari have argued, the symbolic order of modern patriarchal and capitalist culture subjugates youth to various representatives of the patriarchal father, and their resistances must be understood as resistances against this Oedipal father figure and his disciplinary "machines." These resistances (and here Deleuze and Guttiari) echo the hope of Marcuse and of Nietzsche, that a radical release of desires long repressed, in a multiplicity of forms, might usher in a cultural revolution against all Oedipal father figures, whatever form they may take. This was the hope of the counterculture's sexual revolution of the Sixties, that sexual desire, along with desire for community and creative play, could be revolutionary.

Certainly after the Sixties, this more politicized, radical understanding of self-determination began to give way to a more individualistic understanding, associated with the belief that individuals should construct their own truths and values as relatively-autonomous agents of their own making, their own self-production, not as subjects who identity with social movements for change and understand self-determination as a collective process, in which individual and group differences proliferate but within a context in which differences are also woven together in a broad-based movement for democratization of all social spheres. The individualistic discourse of self-determination does not provide a path to such democratization. Instead, it leads to self-dwelling, subjectivism, and an assertion of autonomy from others. In political theory, it has much in common with historic strands of libertarianism in America, as exemplified by the "objectivist" philosophy of Ayn Rand, with its appeal to liminal youth who want to be free of all controls over them. In such form, it hardly seems progressive or democratic. But the individualist discourse on self-determination, as expressed by Grateful Dead fans, did make some important cultural connections that were not just narrowly self-interested. It is perhaps too easy to view discourses of individualistic self-determination among Deadhead fans as unencumbered by concern with the well-being or equity of others, or with efforts to advance a democratic imagination. Take for example the following comments posted on a Grateful Dead online fan forum:

> One reason so many enjoyed Grateful Dead (GD) shows is because they were a piece of the mosaic. Mostly there was something there for everyone and everyone fit in somewhere, everyone pretty much let everyone else do whatever they wanted ... you could be comfortable being yourself at a show no matter who you are or how you look when in so many other parts of society you were not accepted and this could be a reason for the growth of the fan base.

The radical democratic project here is to accept and welcome individual differences with the Deadhead community, and this requires that everyone is made to feel welcome "no matter who you are ..." It also requires a politics of everyday life that sides with those not accepted in mainstream culture, for whatever reason.

A final expression of an individualistic self-determination in the Deadhead community, which has received considerable attention in Dead studies and (somewhat ironically, business management studies) is based on the principle of the democratization of capitalism and rejection of the profit motive as the purpose of a self-determining organization or business. From the outset, and most particularly then, the Dead (as I have already had cause to note) were anti-profit and pro-community. They presented a radically new vision of what a rock band could be, and perhaps what it needed to be if it was to keep the spirit of he counterculture alive, including a radical new imagining of an economy for a counterculture community.

The Deadhead economy found expression in the parking lot, or Shakedown Street scene at Dead concerts where fans could purchase tie-dye t-shirts, pins, posters, and veggie burritos (along with an assortment of drugs). Was the Deadhead culture really as anti-capitalist, anti-commercial as its official philosophy implied, or had it invented (or revived) a form of capitalism with a human face, a kinder and gentler capitalism, a capitalism that reconciles Marx and Adam Smith? Was its anti-commercial ideology little more than a manufactured and marketable image—something that could be used to "brand" the band for a counterculture fan base that wanted to believe in the image. According to Nadya Zimmerman, the Dead performed an "anti-commercial counterculture" image, and however manufactured, this image "would prove to be one of its most marketable commodities ... The Grateful Dead advertised an image of itself as a collection of anti-commercial unprofessionals [and some] were convinced by this image" (Zimmerman, pp. 197–198). This is, of course, a deeply cynical view of the Grateful Dead and Deadhead culture, one in keeping with a recent revisionist history of the counterculture and the Sixties: the supposed ideals of the Sixties counterculture were a sham, hiding the fact that the counterculture never unplugged from either consumer society or capitalism. There is just enough truth to this narrative to make it seem reasonable, and it is usually invoked by way of saying, hey, it's okay to be a capitalist so long as that means supporting a free market, open, even egalitarian form of capitalism envisioned by Adam Smith.

"It was a rebel life: escaping the boredom of a straight job to make cool shirts, sell them at shows, and then fall asleep in a tent reading Karl Marx's economic critiques. Campgrounds instead of corporate offices, tie-dyes instead of neckties, it was an end run around The Man and his materialistic ball and chain. But, of course, the irony is that the attempt to opt out of that capitalist system led directly to the free and open marketplace of capitalism .... Was it what Ben Cohen and Jerry Garcia would later term caring capitalism if none of the profits went to charity, but rather for tickets, gas, and food?... Marx's critique may have been right on the money for the corporate capitalist life I was avoiding, they missed the mark with the eye-to-eye, hand-to-hand, homemade marketplace that was the Dead parking lot scene. It was a kinder, gentler brand of capitalism" (Gimbel and Cushing-Daniels, pp. 3–4). The problem with this argument is that it misrepresents Marx and Marxism. Marx understood capitalism as associated with an increasing concentration of wealth and the rationalization of the social and technical relations of production (as on an assembly line). Marxism indicates that the kind of free market craft and barter society that once existed in Europe and elsewhere, had given way during the rise of capitalism to the industrial revolution and all the great inequalities that followed. As for Adam Smith, he harbored a utopian hope that free market capitalism need not inevitably lead to greater inequality or the oppression of a working class. But history proved him wrong on that count. So what Gimbel and Cushing-Daniels end up arguing is that we can have unrestricted capitalism, as Adam Smith envisioned it, by following the craft industry model of the Dead parking lot. I would argue that this small-scale, craft industry, bartering model is actually pre-capitalism and anti-capitalist, not a "kinder, gentler, version of capitalism." Nevertheless, the question must be asked as to whether this craft industry model is a realistic alternative to mass production industry, or whether it is something that can survive only at the margins. At the very least, the Deadhead craft economy model provides a quite radical critique of mass consumption society, and I believe of capitalism as a system that tends toward monopoly, the concentration of wealth, and the reduction of all human relations to object relations. Gimbel and Cushing-Daniels view these effects of capitalism as associated only with an un-kind, and un-gentle capitalism, one that alienated people from their labor, whether they labor on the assembly line or (like most Deadheads) in the office, where it as "more often than not unclear exactly what the ultimate product was" (p. 9). This was the kind of capitalism that brought us the "military-industrial complex," and suburbia, a "safe but sanitized" space without community. All of those parts of our "species being" Marx believed were suppressed by industrial capitalism—including "individuality" and "creativity"—created the conditions for a counterculture backlash among middle-class youth (p. 9). The hippie movement, the authors argue, ultimately proved to be unsustainable because it was still too closely tied to corporate capitalist work and production—a dubious claim given that the Sixties counterculture created the conditions for the craft economy of Deadhead culture. The correct response, from their perspective, is to embrace capitalism, but capitalism with a human face, capitalism of the Adam Smith variety. The Dead craft economy "was capitalism, pure and simple—literally pure, simple, uncomplicated, non-corporate capitalism" (Gimbel & Cushing-Daniels, p. 11). The problem here is the assumption that capitalism is an ideal, as Adam Smith conceived and described it. But capitalism always has been an historical, emerging, developing phenomenon, and it always has emerged out of cultural struggles, calling into existence the working class that would resist and (Marx believed) finally transcend it through some form of socialism.

Is Deadhead culture more Smith than Marx, and is capitalism to be the grounding of a new counterculture? As I have said, the way to respond to such questions is by interpreting the Deadhead (and Phish) parking lot economies as non-capitalism, even anti-capitalism, to the extent that they do not participate in the exploitation of a working class or alienate workers from the means and the product of their labor. For Marx, a barter economy tied to simple change is not merely an incipient form of capitalism. (See Marx. Economic Manuscripts: Critique of Political Economy, and Capital: Volume One, the first few chapters.) Rather, capitalism represents a fundamental change from an economy in which people are engaged in the production of things that have real "use value," like a tie-dye t-shirt expertly and uniquely crafted and bought at a reasonable price, or exchanged for something of equal use-value, like a couple veggie burritos, hand-crafted by local vegans. Human relations of relative equality are sustained in such an economy, whereas according to Marx capitalism is associated with the making of a highly inequitable society, based on the commodity form—music as a commodity, produced by the music industry to sell, without regard for its quality, or its use-value, how it actually makes people live happier, more connected, more meaningful lives. This is why it is important that the Dead, and Phish, have for the most part kept their distance from the music industry, understanding what harm it would do to their music and to music fans.

References

Dodd, D. (2005). *The complete annotated Grateful Dead lyrics*. New York, NY: Simon & Shuster.
Fowler, C. (2002). *Insiders' guide to Berkeley and the East Bay*. Guilford, CT: Globe Pequot Press.
Gardner, D. et al. (1983). A *nation at risk: the imperative for educational reform. An open letter to the American people. A report to the nation and the secretary of education*. Washington, D.C.: National Commission on Excellence in Education.
Gehr, R., & Phish. (1998). *The Phish book*. New York, NY: Villard.
Heidegger, M., & Stambaugh, J. (1996). *Being and time: A translation of Sein und Zeit*. Albany, NY: State University of New York Press.
Hunter, B. (2000). Interview: Ben "Junta" Hunter. PHISH NET. https://phish.net/blog/1330115828/iv-ben-hunter.html. Retrieved April 10, 2020.
Lesh, P. (2005). *Searching for the sound: My life with the Grateful Dead*. New York, NY: Little, Brown.
McNally, D. (2002). *A Long Strange Trip: The Inside History of the Grateful Dead*. New York: Three Rivers Press.
Meriwether, N. G. (2012). *Reading the Grateful Dead: A critical survey*. Lanham, MD: Scarecrow Press.
Parish, S., & Layden, J. (2003). *Home before daylight: My life on the road with the Grateful Dead*. New York, NY: St. Martin's Press.
Scully, R., & Dalton, D. (1996). *Living with the dead: Twenty years on the bus with Garcia and the Grateful Dead*. Boston, MA: Little, Brown.
Schinder, S., & Schwartz, A. (2008). *Icons of rock: An encyclopedia of the legends who changed music forever*. Westport, CT: Greenwood Press.
Shor, I. (1992). *Culture wars: School and society in the conservative restoration 1969–1984*. Chicago, IL: University of Chicago Press.
Weir, R. (2014), Tie-dye and flannel shirts: the Grateful Dead and the battle over the long sixties. *Journal of Popular Music Studies*, 26: 137–161. doi:10.1111/jpms.12064

About Our Team

Shirley R. Steinberg

This book was built on rock n' roll (I never imagined I would be quoting Starship). As Kent mentioned in his acknowledgments, I wanted to make sure the "Phish" book was published, however, after making the commitment, it was clear that I needed more than a bit of help. Full disclosure: while many will acknowledge that my blood pumps through rock veins, I have often noted there are bands I just don't get...Phish was one of them, and Dennis Carlson knew this. He even noted to me that when I read his book, I would *finally* understand my own lack of cultural awareness. This given, it was a daunting task, to edit and complete a book which was written by the ultimate #1 fan of the damn band. I was determined to assemble a Phish Team. The notion of the rock n' roll academic has only two meanings.... a kick ass scholar who breathes the music in between Foucauldian/Gramscian discourses, *or* a kick ass scholar/musician who alternates breaths between Habermas/Lennon-McCartney/Freire/Brian Wilson/Butler/Dylan. I opted for the latter ass kickers and brought in some big axes. These guys rose to the occasion, Bob Lake (guitar) and Michael MacDonald (every instrument on Earth) moved sentences, verses, filled in gaps and organized the book with their genius and fraternity. I love them both, respect them with abandon, thanking them from my soul. Two dear human beings were our external reviewers, saving my own ass more than once: Phil Anderson (drummer) was my rock conscience, reading the manuscript, advising, and adding his amusement at my Phishy disdain. David Hirschman (guitar), with whom I share my life (as well as my annoyance with Phish), became the bigger man by advising me on the book and discussing the band with me (we both continue to eschew jam bands). Dudes, I'm glad *you enjoy myself*. Mega thanks to the four of you for rocking my world with your fraternity. Love and thanks to Ron Clemons, artist extraordinaire and beloved brother to Denny and Kent. Kent Peterson (vocalist) was my spirit guide, encouraging me with stories or notes about Denny. I remember 3 decades ago, meeting his Denny and observing his continual need to *get home quickly*. He would disappear and phone home (from New York, Glasgow, San Diego…name it), talking incessantly about the farm…he hated being away from Kent… they are a love for the ages. Dennis Carlson, I miss you, managing to force-feed me Phish of all things….you are our rock n' roll shooting star, respected, admired, forever missed.

Our team

Dennis L. Carlson earned a bachelor's degree in 1968 from the University of Washington in editorial journalism. In 1969, he earned his teacher certification at Western Carolina University through the Teacher Corps program. He later returned to the University of Washington in 1972 to complete his master's degree in Urban Planning, with a speciality in Urban Education. He completed his doctorate degree in 1979 at the University of Wisconsin-Madison focusing on Education Policy Studies.

At the time of his death in April 2015, Carlson was Professor of Curriculum, Cultural Studies of Education, and the Social Foundations of Education at Miami University, Oxford, OH. He previously taught at Rutgers University, Hobart & William Smith Colleges and the University of Wisconsin-Madison, as well as serving in the Teacher Corps in Franklin, NC, and the Peace Corps in Libya.

Carlson authored and edited many notable books in the field of curriculum studies. His scholarship focused on issues pertained to teachers' work culture, progressive and democratic education, cultural studies, youth subcultures and gender and sexuality studies in education.

His opus includes the following titles:

Volunteers of America: The Journey of a Peace Corps Teacher
Dennis L. Carlson
Rotterdam: Sense Publishers (2012)
ISBN-10: 9460917356

The Education of Eros: A History of Education and the Problem of Adolescent Sexuality
Dennis L. Carlson
Routledge/Taylor & Francis Group (2012)
ISBN-13: 9780415507516

Leaving Safe Harbors: Toward a New Progressivism in American Education and Public Life
Dennis L. Carlson
Routledge/Falmer, New York, NY (2002)
ISBN-13: 9780415933780
ISBN-10: 0415933781

Power/knowledge/pedagogy: The Meaning of Democratic Education in Unsettling Times
Dennis L. Carlson, Michael W. Apple, Editors
Routledge/Avalon Publishing (1998)
ISBN-13: 978081339026
ISBN-10: 0813390265

Making Progress: Education and Culture in New Times
Dennis L. Carlson
Teachers College Press, Columbia University, New York (1997)
ISBN-13: 978080773577
ISBN-10: 0807735779

Teachers and Crisis: Urban School Reform and Teachers' Work Culture
Dennis L. Carlson
Routledge/Taylor & Francis Group, New York (1992)
ISBN-13: 9780415902700
ISBN-10: 0415902703

Ron Clemons has photographed professionally for the past 16 years. Show venues include Findlay Market, Below Zero Lounge, Starbucks, and Essex Studios in Cincinnati, Ohio. Fortunate to have his works selected for the DIA International Exhibit sponsored by the Center of fine Art Photography, his artwork has also been used to raise monies for non-profits such as The Drop In Center, CCAT and Caracole. His images have been used in book cover designs for local authors, Doug Cooper Spencer and most recently, the late Dennis Carlson. He photographed The AIDS Walk with STOP AIDS, Caracole's Spring Grove Walk/Run, Caracole's Annual Meeting, Tall Stacks Cincinnati, The Opening Ceremony for The Underground Freedom Center, and was Photographer for the Cincinnati Men's Chorus for their 2017 Concert Season. He was part of the Exhibit, Manifestions of Time: The Black Experience, sponsored by Mohawk Galleries located in Cincinnati in 2019. Ron believes photography reminds us that we are surrounded by beauty. Our task is to find the angle and perspective that invites that beauty into the framework of our spirit. ron722@aol.com

Note from Kent Peterson about Ron Clemons:
I was the first conductor of the Cinti Men's Chorus and Ron was elected as the first President of the Board of CMC. Through many meetings, rehearsals and a few cocktails following those encounters, we struck up a friendship which has through the years evolved into brotherhood, that is how Denny came to know Ron. Eventually, they began taking annual trips to Chicago every May to attend the International Mr. Leather contests, something I could never do as I was still teaching school & couldn't get away. Through many shared holidays and shared life experiences; we were gay men facing the carnage and personal loss foist upon us by the AIDS epidemic and fighting bigotry on the civil rights front…we became true brothers. When I was visiting my folks in Phoenix, Denny called to tell me I had to come home immediately as he had awakened that morning unable to walk, I called Ron to be with him until I could arrange my travel to get home. He is indeed our brother from another mother.

Editors:

Robert Lake is Professor at Georgia Southern University. He teaches undergraduate and graduate courses in curriculum studies and multicultural education. Robert is the author of *Vygotsky on Education* (Peter Lang Publishing, 2012) and *A Curriculum of Imagination in an Era of Standardization: An Imaginative Dialogue with Maxine Greene and Paulo Freire* (Information Age, 2013). A former garage band guitar and harmonica player, he has written about music in education and taught English to refugees and undocumented migrant workers through songs.

Michael B. MacDonald is an award-winning filmmaker and associate professor of music at the MacEwan University Faculty of Fine Arts and Communications in Edmonton, Alberta, Canada. His research areas include popular music scenes, screen production research, community-engaged ethnographic film theory. Michael is the founding program chair of the MusCan Film Series held annually at the Canadian University Music Society conference, serves on the editorial board of the journal Intersections, the program committee for KISMIF an international conference on DIY culture, member of the scientific committee for combArt, and an active member of the International Council of Traditional Music Study Group on Audiovisual Ethnomusicology. Michael is also the cofounder of Justice4Reel, a community media activism free school.

Shirley R. Steinberg considers herself the ultimate devotee of rock n' roll. Her first *grown-up* concert was The Righteous Brothers in 1965… however, it was the opening act of Buffalo Springfield that changed her life. Unable to make money as a musician or as a fan, she is a research professor of Critical Youth studies at the University of Calgary, Canada…a site visited by Dennis Carlson because he didn't believe that any place could be that cold or that boring. The author of numerous books and articles, she spends her free time attending concerts and still trying to figure Phish out. She is the executive director of freireproject.org and an advocate for refugee and immigrant education. The mother of four adult children, she attempted to ensure their own devotion to music and fed them Zepplin, the Beatles, and a plethora of musical theatre from birth. Continually wondering *what's goin' on*, she shares her life with a kick-ass rock n'roll, rockabilly, jazz strumming guitarist.

Studies in Criticality

General Editor
Shirley R. Steinberg

Counterpoints publishes the most compelling and imaginative books being written in education today. Grounded on the theoretical advances in criticalism, feminism, and postmodernism in the last two decades of the twentieth century, Counterpoints engages the meaning of these innovations in various forms of educational expression. Committed to the proposition that theoretical literature should be accessible to a variety of audiences, the series insists that its authors avoid esoteric and jargonistic languages that transform educational scholarship into an elite discourse for the initiated. Scholarly work matters only to the degree it affects consciousness and practice at multiple sites. Counterpoints' editorial policy is based on these principles and the ability of scholars to break new ground, to open new conversations, to go where educators have never gone before.

For additional information about this series or for the submission of manuscripts, please contact:

> Shirley R. Steinberg
> c/o Peter Lang Publishing, Inc.
> 29 Broadway, 18th floor
> New York, New York 10006

To order other books in this series, please contact our Customer Service Department:

> peterlang@presswarehouse.com (within the U.S.)
> orders@peterlang.com (outside the U.S.)

Or browse online by series:
> www.peterlang.com